The Most Rebellious Town in Devon

by Colin Haynes

Arthritis Care

For every copy of this book sold at the cover price, a donation will be made to help the work of this charity.

Published by ColyPublications,
Colyton, EX24 6PG

ISBN 0-9546432-0-8

Formatted and printed by Creeds the Printers, Broadoak, Bridport DT6 5NL

Cover design by the author and created by John Forrester-Addie.
Inside illustrations by John Forrester-Addie and Mary Panter
unless otherwise acknowledged.

AUTHOR'S NOTE

My particular interest in this period of Colyton's history was due entirely to stumbling across a reference in official Chantry (church) records, which read:

"Colyton......... The Most Rebellious Town in Devon".

What notoriety this gave the town and the discovery of such a dramatic phrase led to a period of research to discover its origins. It has resulted in this work of "faction" – a modern word that seems most suited – which sets out to tell a story during a momentous time in Colyton's history.

Whilst there is a great number of academic and fictitious works on the rebellion, I feel justified in adding to the list as it offers a local focus not previously attempted. This book in no way claims to be an academic work, rather an attempt by the author to bring together known facts and recorded opinions from a wide variety of sources.

The names and events referred to are historically accurate – opinion, imagination and embellishment, have, by necessity, been employed in order to create and weave a story about the town and people of Colyton. *Unless otherwise stated every person referred to was a Colyton citizen who conducted the trade ascribed to them.* Dialogue in italics has been created by the author whilst the execution speeches were those recorded at the time and believed to be accurately attributed.

For anyone wishing to pass on information or watch progress please look at www.monmouthrebellion.co.uk or write to me at the address shown on the facing page.

Colin Haynes

FOLK BALLAD OF 1692

Oh Lord where is my husband now
Where once he stood beside me?

His body lies at Sedgemoor
In grave of oak and ivy;

Come tell me you who beat the drum,
Why am I so mistreated?

To stand alone a traitor's wife,
My will to live defeated.

He swore to me he would be gone
For days but two and twenty –

And yet in seven years or more
His bed lies cold and empty.

The scars upon my body have grown cold;
To spin the broken remnants of my soul.

Oh Lord where is my husband now
Where once he stood beside me?

My Thanks

For the help and patience of Helen, local librarian par excellence, John for encouragement and reading my mind to produce the drawing interpretations, Dr Pam Sharpe for her invaluable historic input and correction, Jane for patience and support often stretched to the limits but still providing the essential encouragement when doubts set in. Mary, another Colin and Carol for typesetting skill and patience.

CONTENTS

INTRODUCTION

The headline-grabbing title of this book has its roots in dissent and non-conformity and formed the basis of the Duke of Monmouth's claim to the Crown of England, his landing at Lyme Regis and the honest men of Colyton who saw no alternative but to rebel in 1685.

This book sets out to record real people and real events which took place in Colyton's streets and within some houses still standing to this very day – if only their walls could speak what secrets could be uncovered! Colyton's ancient street pattern has remained unchanged over the centuries and certainly the layout seen today was just so at the time of this tale.

In trying to build a picture of their lives and the conditions in which they lived it can certainly be presumed many of their experiences reflect how things were in other towns and villages of Devon, Dorset and Somerset. The atmosphere, experiences and attitudes being explored within these pages would have been similar throughout the valleys and neighbouring communities. Their populations were joined through marriage, trade and friendship, which provided a connection between many families in the area. For this reason a brief look will also be taken at the names of those rebels who participated from Axmouth, Beer, Colyford, Seaton, Musbury, Whitford and Kilmington, at the end of the book.

The Monmouth Rebellion of 1685 caused such an effect on the small community of Colyton, with a quarter of the male population leaving their homes to join this 'last rebellion on English soil'. This major period of unrest, albeit brief, was to upset Colyton, and other tight-knit rural communities beyond measure. A series of quite horrible events came down upon them, which would leave their mark on not only the town, but on all of East Devon for many years to come.

My research started with a complete list of all the Colyton men who became directly involved in the fateful event and actually marched off with Monmouth. Next was to discover some of their experiences and finally what became of them. Some records and documentation during this period were well kept and provide detailed insights, once uncovered.

One hundred and five Colyton men, more I believe, than any other town in

Devon, joined the Duke of Monmouth in rebellion against 'the papist Crown of England'. Fourteen of them would eventually face the hangman – two actually in Colyton – and 22 were transported to the West Indies and ten years of slavery.

The 17th century saw the English throne occupied by six different monarchs and was a period that produced considerable drama and suffering for Colyton. There was a major harvest failure in 1631, which led to the start of a textile depression. The town found itself the centre of activity between opposing forces during the Civil War of 1642 (first occupied by Royalist forces and then by Cromwell's army) whilst the plague of 1646 had caused the death of over 20% of the population. Families, and indeed the labour force, were still recovering from these effects.

To understand the unfolding events of 1685, it is necessary to look in some detail at the repression faced by the population. Colyton, like much of East Devon, was a key centre of dissent and as you read, it's particularly interesting to learn of the major part played in this by Colyton's Chamber of Feoffees. At varying times they found themselves supporting non-conformity, aiding the poor and were eventually required to supervise hangings in their town.

To me, one thing became absolutely clear; the people of whom you will read were religious and God-fearing men and women. All they wanted was to worship on their terms, in their own way and have an independence of life and spirit.

If you are interested in a more detailed and in depth study of Colyton I recommend you read 'Population and Society in an East Devon Parish' by Pamela Sharpe (University of Exeter Press ISBN 0 85989 655 2)

CHRONOLOGICAL TABLE

6th Feb 1685	Death of Charles II. Duke of York inherits throne
1st June	Duke of Monmouth sets sail from Holland
11th June	Duke of Monnouth lands at Lyme
12th June	Training of the gathering volunteer force
15th June	The rebel army marches to Axminster
18th June	Monmouth's forces enter Taunton
19th June	Monmouth persuaded to be proclaimed King
21st June to 4th July	The rebel army marches through Somerset
5th July	Monmouth persuaded to mount night attack on Royalist camp
5/6th July	Battle of Sedgemoor fought during the hours of darkness
6th July	Rebel army defeated, routed and pursued ruthlessly
8th July	Monmouth captured in Dorset
15th July	Monmouth beheaded on Tower Hill
5th Sept	Judge Jeffreys Dorchester Assize opens
14th Sept	Exeter Assize opens
17th Sept	Hangings in Colyton
18th Sept	Taunton Assize opens
22nd Sept	Wells Assize opens
24th Nov	Colyton rebel prisoners embark ship for Barbados
8th Jan 1686	Colyton rebels arrive in Barbados
March	General Pardon announced
9th May 1687	John Whicker and Peter Bagwell escape captivity
June 1688	John Whicker and Peter Bagwell arrive home
May 1689	Petition to King William on behalf of rebels

16ᵗʰ and 17ᵗʰ CENTURY BACKGROUND

The southwest had long been a prosperous region with the area between Salisbury, Exeter and Bristol having far more relative importance in the country than today. There was greater stability and more wealth enjoyed here than in many other parts of England.

Agriculture and the cloth trade were at the forefront of these earnings, bringing considerable prosperity to the area, and people's lives had become much improved. As time moved on, ever increasing numbers worked for wages, rather than just their keep on an estate, providing them with an independence of others. Large numbers of workers were well established and involved as weavers, cloth finishers, dyers and combers. The wool trade produced thick broadcloths and lighter serge, which were in demand and sold throughout Europe.

There can be no clearer example of Colyton's wealth than the lantern tower sitting proudly atop the Parish Church of St Andrew. This magnificent addition was built in the fifteenth century funded by those enjoying the profits from the wool trade. In the opinion of some, its design and style was influenced by that seen in Belgium and brought back by those merchants who travelled and traded there.

Colyton's main participation was in the work of dyeing and finishing of cloth after it had been collected and later redistributed from Exeter for the next stages of its production. It was this trade that saw the building of fulling and tucking mills on the River Coly and drying racks on the common and even on the church green! One such spot is recorded as 'Rack Green' situated

St Andrew's Church

between the town and Colcombe Castle★. Cloth was hung on a wooden tenterframe and stretched with hooks after bleaching and fulling but before teasing and cropping★★. Large numbers of men were also employed as weavers of serge and cloth, often as part time to other employment. It was a common sight to see a loom in the corner of many a kitchen or parlour.

Using profits from their trades, men sought to achieve land ownership or holding a lease, and this self-employment of the day encouraged greater effort, harder work and better productivity. Unfortunately it was the time of land being taken up by the larger farming enterprises and it was getting increasingly difficult to find small plots or fields to buy. This is demonstrated by the 71 acres of manorial land in the ownership of yeoman Peter Bagwell but in parcels spread over a wide area of the parish, whilst on the other hand Roger Satchell held good wealth in cash but only had an estate worth £20, indicating how he had found it difficult to invest profits, from successful trading, in land.

A benefit of ownership confirmed the right to vote at vestry meetings, which provided some participation in local government. The downside of this, for the likes of yeomen, innkeepers, clothiers, farmers and tradesmen, came with the 'privilege' of paying rates. Eventually they would have the right to elect a member to parliament. The local squire was normally the Justice of the Peace and administered the law on petty matters and he could also overrule vestry decisions or change appointed officers. His local qualifications were substantial landed property, ability to read and write and some knowledge of Latin. At Quarter Sessions he would sit with others to try more serious matters and was the linchpin of English government.

Thus had developed a thriving and assertive community where clothiers, dyers and tuckers were in many ways no less important than some of the gentry. They, together with farmers, tradesmen and smallholders, formed an urban middle class that was strongly non-conformist.

It seems women played a large part in the running of small businesses with some organising the lacemaking labour locally for the merchants who

---

★ Almost certainly this was just on the town side of Umborne Bridge where the Tool Box is today. It makes it likely the local given name of 'green bridge' comes from this.

★★ The origin of our phrase of 'being on tenterhooks'.

purchased finished goods, which meant they too were accustomed to having firm opinions of their own in many cases. At different times in Colyton the lace trade provided an income for upwards of 300, many of whom were children sent out to lace schools as young as five years old. In later years, as desires for education grew, they were taught to read as well as make lace by the dame who kept the school. Boys as well as girls worked for up to twelve hours a day in summer whilst the light was good. Grown men also made lace as a sideline in their evenings and often they were sailors back from long voyages and not yet signed on for another vessel. For many single women it provided just enough income to cover their rent and have a degree of independence.

It is widely accepted that Flemish refugees introduced the lace skills during Queen Elizabeth's reign. Established first in Honiton it then spread to most parishes in the East Devon area by the latter part of the seventeenth century. The Low Countries of Europe were strongly anti catholic so connections of this nature help one to understand how regular contacts with the Continent existed and must have helped the spread of dissent and non-conformist views.

Colyton's success in the wool trade and agriculture in the sixteenth century had made it a town of real commercial importance in Devon, being the fourth largest contributor of taxes in the county. This is demonstrated by the list of wealthiest towns in 1543 measured by revenue collected from all lay persons whose real or personal estate amounted to more than £40 a year. Perhaps to be expected, Exeter's was the greatest with a recorded figure of sixty contributions totalling £6,250 followed by 30 from Totnes amounting to £2,965, Plymouth only a surprising third with 15 contributors totalling £1,734, **Colyton 12 assessments amounting to £660,** followed by Ottery and Tavistock.

Around this time all was not perfect and the parish was to experience a major event with considerable social repercussions. In 1539 Henry Courtenay, Marquis of Exeter, then head of the family and Lord of the Manor, fell out with his kinsman, Henry VIII, resulting in his incarceration in The Tower, confiscation of all his lands and eventual execution by beheading – hanging being for the lower ranks! From Norman times it was the Courtenay family in whose hands the lands of Colyton had been vested after they had come over from France around 1151.

The prosperity we have spoken of could not have taken place without considerable organisation and administration of local affairs. However, the absence of a Lord of the Manor had left a gap in discipline and regulation of community matters. Whilst merchants and traders got quietly on with their business there was no head person to take your problems to or seek to resolve disputes regarding land or domesticity. There were many matters requiring sound judgement and leadership but it was now clearly lacking.

Such a structure was of importance so, after much discussion, a group of merchants and yeomen got together and decided to try and buy back the lands from the King. It was 1546 and they had heard Henry was short of funds for his wars and shipbuilding so, if the time was chosen carefully, a good chance of success might exist.

This required great courage and bravery to make such an audacious and bold approach to the King and especially one known for his unpredictability and outbursts of temper. Put this together with the very nature and dangers of a journey to London and you begin to get a picture of what faced the group. Apart from those in trade or on government business very few people travelled any distance in those days and even Honiton was visited by few and only rarely. Thus they had chosen to embark on a major adventure facing along the way risks from highwaymen and other dangers presented along the dusty tracks.

Raising as much as they could between them put 1,000 marks at their disposal but would it be enough? Thus twenty-five men and two women, Edith Strowbridge and Alicia Tycon (of the fulling mill at Nunsford), set off on their hazardous task uncertain of getting there, unsure of success but with a belief and commitment worthy of England's finest.

Arriving in London they faced delays, uncertainty and promises of an audience and several days passed without seeing the King. Boredom, anxiety and fears grew as they sat around waiting for the call. Finally, when summoned into the monarch's presence their pleas and proposition was offered with great eloquence. Further days of waiting followed whilst the monarch deliberated and sought guidance from his advisers. Eventually, to their relief and joy, a decision in their favour was forthcoming.

From this 'the twenty' were enfeoffed★ by this terrible King and in so doing were granted land and property together with the management of the fair and markets and the income from them. 'The rents and income from the manor to be expended in such good, godly and commendable uses as they should determine'.

Also granted was a court of Pie Powder★★ and hence they became a complete parochial corporation with whom and to whom by common consent, all the machinery of the town, short of the administration of the law, seemed to devolve.

Thus had been born the Chamber of Feoffees, a corporation consisting of 12 Feoffees and twenty freeholders elected by the parishioners. From Colyton's viewpoint this resulted in the establishment of the first form of local government. Life would now settle into an organised style, an example of which was the early start of a grammar school in 1599.

The old 'Church House' still stands proudly in the Market Place to this very day and here in a first-floor chamber the Feoffees' meetings took place. Part of their responsibilities included the provision of a guard for the King or his representatives whenever called upon. To this end it had been necessary to establish an armoury of guns, powder and swords. As with everything else they had done this was provided in a most efficient manner.

★   the instrument or deed by which one is invested the fee of an estate.

★★ First granted in the medieval period by kings charter for small towns and villages to preside over markets and fairs. It was responsible for settling disputes on site between buyers and sellers, make judgements concerning quality of goods and check 'weights & Measures'. It was presided over by a man of some standing and known as the Steward. Market disputes could quickly fall into a riot if no controls were present. The expression 'pie-powder' is derived from old French 'pied-pouldre' which translated means dusty footed which some suggest is in reference to a court held on open ground rather than under a roof.

The Colyton Chamber of Feoffees still has in its possession the original Charter and the names of the first twenty are acknowledged each year at an annual banquet in their memory. In the twenty-first century, as a body, they continue to meet and play an important role in the community to this very day. Names of their members in the original list include Bagwell, Basleigh, Blackmore, Marwood, Newton and Whicker of whom family members appear on our list of rebels.

It must have been the very apparent success and regained stability of Colyton and the availability of a fresh water supply within the town that attracted the Yonge family to establish a mansion home by building The Great House

during the years of 1550-1580. It was a most picturesque building of much larger proportions than we see today possibly having been cut down as a result of damage during the Civil War. Entrance was from Cuckoo Street (known to us as South Street) through an elliptical arch set in flint and many fine features were contained in its

The Great House

interior. Their position and wealth allowed them to take the north aisle of St Andrew's Church as the family burial place which places them as supporters of the established church and only in the next generation does this seem to publicly change.

It was Walter Yonge who wrote the well acclaimed political diaries during the period 1604-28 in Colyton★ and showed the strength of stern puritan convictions and abhorrence of dancing and plays.

England was divided into nine thousand parishes. Accompanying this were legal controls created to enforce obedience to the government and preserve a form of society. The parish council bore the ecclesiastical name of the vestry and was presided over by the rector. It consisted of various unpaid officers including churchwardens, overseers of the poor, the constable and

★   they were much acclaimed and published by The Camden Society in 1848

surveyor of the high roads. Each was nominated annually by the ratepayers and confirmed by the justice of the peace. One law strongly enforced was the control of labourers who were not permitted to stray from their parish boundary into another for work and any caught so trying would be punished at the whipping post or stocks.

Another example of Colyton having been a place of strong independence of both view and action was its opposition to taxation. During the time of 'Ship Money' levies (1634-40) within the county of Devon the east had 445 (51%) defaulters of which Colyton produced sixty nine, the second largest to Cullompton! Opposition to this tax was led by the diarist Sir Walter Yonge so clearly, even then, respectable and successful merchants had no wish to part with their hard earned money in taxes!

Since the 1670s a wind of insecurity had gathered caused by rising prices, competition with French manufacturers and growing unemployment. The war against the Dutch had resulted in disruption to their export trade and competition of cheaper cloth from other areas was beginning to have an effect. Newly invented looms began to create unemployment with some capable of doing the work of 20 men. Hitherto the South West's cloth trade had been the foundation of the country's foreign trading bringing with it the social development we have spoken of, much ahead of elsewhere in the country.

Most land belonged to large farmers who sent substantial production to market and provided a yeoman elite. However, a general undermining of confidence and bad feelings were rapidly developing, partly due to previously mentioned land shortages for the less well off. Everything was given even greater impetus by the increasing war being waged against dissenters with whom increasing numbers of workers sympathised or were to be found firmly amongst their ranks. Undoubtedly this helped goad wage earners into protest and began to generate very real potential for uprising of which the Duke of Monmouth became the figurehead.

As is apparent throughout history any revolutionary period inevitably increases the number of people who become drawn into an active interest and involvement with politics that would not normally have done so. Now this became particularly evident in the yeoman and middle classes who were fast showing dissatisfaction with political and religious affairs both of which had become inseparable. As a result the middle classes discovered allies above and below their ranks with puritan squires and gentlemen, of whom there were many in the southwest, beginning a call to unite for 'liberty and the Protestant Religion' and campaigning for a new parliament – from this grew 'The New Country Party'.

During this time many men in the West Country maintained a contact with London and elsewhere by a correspondence system connecting radical Baptists with City meeting houses where like-minded groups met regularly. In 1672 Charles II issued a Declaration of Indulgence. Licences were issued to dissenting ministers and meeting houses were permitted, including two in Colyton. Even though this Declaration was withdrawn the following year dissenting speakers continued to preach.

Within the parish of Colyton a social hierarchy existed with the establishment of the successful middling class of skill and trades. Payments made to lower workers were very low and often they found themselves forced to accept food or goods in lieu of their wage. There was a level of poverty and many needed considerable help. Pamela Sharpe explained how the Feoffees formed a collection of small dwellings with gardens, which were rented at 4 shillings or less a year. A single woman lace worker, the maintainance being carried out by the chamber, could easily cover such a low amount. Some family papers referred to leases on the 'waste' or common and on one such plot was a home just fourteen feet in length, suggesting it was little more than a hut.

It was the distribution of assistance that provided one way of control being exercised by authority. For both the main church and amongst puritan congregations, looking after the poor offered them the opportunity to increase their numbers and exert control. If indeed parish relief were conditional upon church attendance then the overseers of the poor would be instructed to withhold help from those not complying. Roger Satchell and John Gould, overseers of the poor, had considerable influence in their hands with the most substantial funds of some £235 to distribute in the parish. However, in 1682 questions were raised over their impartiality as both had refused to provide money for some people despite orders from the justices to do so. Action like this indicate the level of power they believed in their possession and how Roger Satchell saw himself of great importance and influence in the community - of both these men we'll hear much more later.

LIFE IN COLYTON AROUND 1680

So what was life like for a resident of the town whose population at this period was some 1,500 living in 237 homes? It makes an interesting comparison with today's figures of 2,800 and 1,150. Join us as we try to create a picture of how life was, how the town would have looked and bring alive some real men and families to introduce to you.

The horse was of course king, and apart from walking, the only means of transport between communities. They worked the fields and pulled the ploughs, toiling like the men who worked long hours at agriculture, wool and cloth trades or lace making. Locally, the landowners of large estates such as those of Shute, Stedcombe and Wiscombe provided employment but opportunities had begun to exist whereby it had become possible for independent earnings to be achieved from small strips of land and other skills. However, there was an increasing trend across Devon for land to be absorbed into larger farms which led to increasing frustrations for those seeking to enhance their position with small holdings.

In residence at The Great House was Sir Walter Yonge the third baronet (1653-1731), which serves to heighten our interest considerably. He sat as MP for Honiton and entertained Monmouth during his 'Progress' through Somerset, Dorset and Devon in 1680. By this time the Yonge family was extremely well established and a most influential force in Colyton. Occupying such a large manor house and the principal one of the town they would have employed a good number of local people as servants, all of whom would be influenced by their employer. Sir Walter, a member of the gentry and, like his father, a stern puritan, was in a position to have been able to encourage a willingness to commit to Monmouth and the rebel cause. It was written of him in 1678 that 'he was a young man of sober conversation and by the part counted as a fanatick. His family well ordered, himself praying in it, morning and evening'.

As now, the church dominated the town with its size and physical presence and even today it is this that impresses many a visitor to this small town. Just imagine it in relation to the community of the seventeenth century, which will help to illustrate the dominant and important nature of the church in their lives. As will be understood this was a time of religious fervour and for some men they would even rather be seen praying at a street corner than not at all.

St Andrew's Church

Travelling back 350 years, what of the trades and businesses of our townsfolk and their means of achieving the independent living we've referred to? Let's look at a few of those of whom we know something and who would take up arms to follow Monmouth. There was Francis Bagwell, sergeweaver★; his brothers John a cordwainer★ and Peter a yeoman★; Ormond Barratt, soapboiler; John Clapp, mercer★; William Clegg, weaver; Phillip Cox, husbandman★ and yeoman; Richard Daniel, tailor; Zachary Drover, joiner; William Greenaway, worsted comber; Nicholas Hoare, tanner; William Marther, carpenter; George Robertson, broadweaver; John Skiffes, shoemaker; Richard Wilmott, mason; and there was the town doctor Nicholas Thompson.

One particular insight illustrating the level of success possible to achieve is that of yeoman John Marwood of 'Blamphayne', Colyton, for whom an inventory of around 1671 exists: three hogsheads of cider, thirty empty hogsheads and three beer barrels, a butter and malt chamber. Stored in the barn was £5 worth of linen, £40 of hay and £90 of wheat, barley and oats. He had 170 ewes and wethers (rams) and 63 lambs, oxen worth £24, 21 cows and a bull valued at £66. Additionally there were 45 barren beasts and young cattle worth £100 and 13 calves worth £8. He also had mares, a nag, colts and poultry. He had at least ten labourers to work on the farm, since he had ten beds in the various chambers. This list is, to say the least, impressive and yet here was a man of whom no more is known than that he followed his belief

---

★ Sergeweaver: weaver of wool to make cloth; cordwainer: a person who makes shoes and supplies his community. From Spanish a worker in Cordovan leather; yeoman: a small freeholder, someone of position in the town but below the gentry; mercer: a merchant or dealer in quality cloth; husbandman: one whose business is to plough and cultivate the land.

and marched with Monmouth. So strong was his belief that he was prepared to leave all the activities and responsibility of his farm to others whilst he went off for an unknown period. By doing so he was placing everything he had achieved and worked for at risk. Some might suggest his success had faltered in the changing economy, which allowed him to feel he had much less to lose.

There were many other merchants and traders meeting the different needs of the community and of course large numbers of yeoman farmers owning or renting parcels of land of varying sizes from which they earnt a living. Those making most success sought constantly to buy more parcels whenever the chance was offered albeit scattered throughout the parish. Surprisingly, small craft businesses such as goldsmiths and pewter workers flourished indicating a capacity and demand to acquire luxury items. More basically, there were plumbers, carpenters, glaziers, blacksmiths, wheelwrights, shoemakers, tailors, tallow chandlers★, saddlers, masons, candlemakers and cordwainers. Tanning was also important with what is now the last oak bark tannery in Britain, in King Street, tanning pits behind Chantry Cottage and a tan works at Puddlebridge. A by-product was soapboiling, coming from the tallow. Pawnbroking also had its place in the local society with button maker Nathaniel Sweet acting as such. All the other skills required to keep this thriving community supplied were to be found.

There were large numbers of Cider orchards with an abundance of apples needing pressing to keep the workers and labourers content. The drink was nothing like we know today as it was produced quickly and in a most rough fashion. Almost every farm carried on cheese making and butter production, some of which were most substantial enterprises.

There may well have been six fulling mills along the Coly, of which most were in the area of Puddlebridge, and nine racks for drying wool, many of which are referred to as being on Colyton Common. Farmers sent their wool to market which was bought either by a comber or spinner who produced the yarn for the weavers. The resulting cloth was sold to the clothier or mercer who processed it at the fullers mill and dyers vat. From here it was sent to Bristol, London or other ports bound for the Continent.

★   Tallow chandler: dealer in the hard fat from cattle or sheep used to make candles, soap or lubricants.

Artist impressions, created from available records and information, showing how Colyton's Market Place may have looked at this time

Zachary Drover had moved to 'Higher Paper Mill' indicating he may have moved from life as a carpenter to another occupation. As paper was made from rags there is a connection with the cloth trade but it was a poor quality paper used by storekeepers for wrapping thread, tobacco and other goods. Colonial imports of tobacco into Lyme Regis encouraged widespread use of the pipe, often by women, and was cheap enough for most to use. Daniel Toupe was involved in this trade as a cutter of the imported product and the resulting tobacco was sold in local shops and by pedlars, making it readily available in Colyton. Inns and drinking houses played a large part in business activities of many local women. Not only did they buy and sell in these houses, it seems they served liquor and drank in them for pleasure. From this, one concludes there existed a definite assertiveness and involvement of women at all levels, including the organising of labour and running businesses. Perhaps this was in part due to many women being left widows after the Civil War, forty years earlier, and who doubtless had to find ways to support themselves and their children. Evidence suggests that women were quite prepared to take a lead in protest against government and authority which probably meant some were most influential in deciding to send their men folk off with the rebels.

On leaving the town boundaries, which were close in to the centre, the rural lanes were more hedge lined than today, with dozens of what we now call green lanes criss crossing the landscape, providing easy routes between farms and rural communities. There were five roads or tracks into town, including what we now know as South Street, which was farmland as soon as the town centre was left behind. Neither bridge existed and instead the river was probably crossed by fords for packhorses with, perhaps, a rickety old footbridge alongside.

The street pattern has remained unchanged and many of the old buildings remain, albeit their façades and rooflines have changed with fashion. Much of what we see today has its roots in those bygone days. It's hard to imagine that all the streets were just dirt surfaces, dusty in summer and a mud bath at times during the winter months. Walking the streets on a winter's night, and with a little imagination, it's quite possible to take your mind back over 300 years.

Many of the buildings were timbered and single storey with roofs of thatch

but over the years fire destroyed them (often repeatedly) and as time progressed safer materials were gradually introduced after such incidents. Substantial properties were built by the more successful merchants indicating the wealth gained by those acting as mercers or agents for the sale and distribution of manufactured cloth, wools and lace. In this capacity they would have dealt with the centre of the European wool market in Antwerp and also traded elsewhere on the Continent. Building styles seen on these travels would inspire and, for some, be brought into use back here.

To provide the reader with a reasonable chance to identify locations referred to let us relate them to shops or buildings well known today. For instance, in the area of South Square was a cluster of thatched houses and water pump or fountain. Below this square was the first holding tank for fresh water serving the town. Around what we call Hillhead, just a road ending in a track leading up out of town, were more thatched properties and in buildings such as these the various local crafts and trades already mentioned were practised.

Looking down from the square there was the town leat running alongside the street (on the side of Spar) with low, old buildings fronting. A few yards on, where today stands the Town Hall was the Shambles or Market House. This was referred to as the Chamelles in the deed passing it into the management of the Feoffees. Traditionally, an open fronted building where traders could set up their stalls (most commonly those selling meat or fish and often associated with slaughterhouses, of which there were three in the area bounded by the Market Place, Queen Street and Church Street).

Squeezed in behind was the Red Lion Inn of which there's more to hear as the story progresses. On the other side of the road were some half-timbered houses owned by merchants and others of moderate means.

The Feoffees held the rights to run a weekly Market and enjoy the profits after rent paid to the crown. In front and alongside the building now known as The Colcombe Castle, stalls would be set out and from the surrounding area would be brought in the widest selection of produce you can imagine, including, cheeses, eggs, butter, cider and cloth for sale or exchange. Extra colour and excitement on these days was added by visiting pedlars offering goods, not normally available for some; travelling minstrels might also visit.

Under another of the licences granted by Henry VIII fairs were held in May and October each year. These were important events in the calendar providing the opportunity to buy and sell livestock, horses, equipment, grain and the like. The Market Place would be packed with enclosures and pens for animals together with crowds drawn from miles around hoping to do business of one kind or another. The drinking houses would be packed to capacity and probably a travelling jester or entertainer would be found visiting.

There is some debate as to whether the stone pillars, seen today at the entrance to the car park, provided a rear access to the Great House for use by tradesmen and others.

Small cottages, shops and workrooms lined much of the Market Place but the wide fronted premises now occupied by Whytes Estate Agency offers evidence of being built and owned by a man of some prosperity in the late fifteenth century or early sixteenth century. Situated directly opposite was the old 'Church House', one of Colyton's oldest and most important buildings after the Church and Vicarage. It stands proud to this day with pinnacled gables and it was here they established the first school in 1599. The schoolmaster lived on the premises and a schoolroom was at the rear. The upper floor provided the guild chamber for the Feoffees as their meeting place and armoury. A 'Muster Master' was employed to supervise the storage of muskets and barrels of powder.

Colyton's Vicarage

As you look at the older buildings in the adjoining streets there are so many that had their origins at the time of our story. The Vicarage dates from at least 1546 and its walls would have heard much talk of the political and religious upheavals over the centuries.

Lower Church Street was crowded with tiny homes and those now rendered would surely have had simple stone facings with thatched roofs, most often of small proportions yet housing several children with room for a loom still found. Outside their front doors women would sit on rickety old stools during daylight hours with a lace-making pillow upon the lap whilst neighbours worked a spinning wheel. Inside some might be heard the beat of a serge-makers loom. Most could not afford to buy the raw material so it was brought to them for finishing, later to be collected by a mercer who would transport and trade them on to others for shipping out from the ports at Lyme, Exeter and Bristol. Sometimes the Feoffees would help finance such purchases of material and in this way helped enable people to achieve earnings for themselves.

The cottages in Queen Square called The Court Houses probably formed one long hall house and in it the Lords of the Manor would hold the Court Leet* dealing with the social, economic and other disputes of the population.

On the corner of Sidmouth Road is Colyton Cottage where one legend suggests Judge Jeffreys stayed a night as he travelled between Dorchester via Lyme to Exeter – disappointingly no evidence seems to exist for this.

The old Court House today

Just past the junction with Church Street and fronting Queen Street is a row of old cottages with a door in the wall. Behind here was the old Quaker burial ground and one of these cottages may well have been the home of Widow Dwight, one of only two people ever licensed to hold prayer meetings during the periods of persecution.

From comments made of the poor condition of the roads and trackways serving Colyton it would appear their maintainance was sadly neglected. Were the Feoffees charged with their responsibility it begs the question that it may have been a self chosen attempt to remain as isolated from authority

---

*   Court Leet was a manorial court held once or twice a year to try petty offences and elect constables and other officers to administer the town's daily affairs.

as possible. Perhaps instead they chose to concentrate on more directly beneficial services such as bringing in a fresh water supply from Ridgeway to a holding tank and then by leats into the town centre. This also made possible the establishment of the first fire brigade in the country circa 1640.

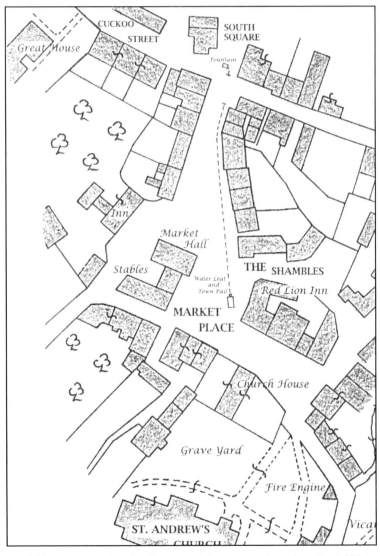

Old estate map showing how town layout may have been in 1685

DISSENT and NON-CONFORMITY

By looking back at the sixteenth and early seventeenth centuries it becomes easier to understand the increasing dissent caused by the religious and political pressures being heaped upon the population of England.

During the sixteenth century, multitudes of English Christians were demanding reform in their church. They sensed it had become corrupt and selfish, and departed from the simple message of the Bible. Social and political changes led people to want more participation in their church. Whilst rulers in the sixteenth century sought to reform the Church of England to some extent, none went far enough to satisfy those who wanted to return to the simple teachings and practices of the Bible.

One militant group within the Church of England genuinely desired to recover biblical teachings and practices. Deeply influenced by the reforms of John Calvin, they became known as "Puritans", perhaps because they insisted upon more purity of doctrine and practice in the church.

Another group seeking reform was called 'Separatists' most of whom were frustrated Puritans who had given up hope of reforming the church from within. They decided to separate from the Church of England and form their own independent congregations. By 1600, there were already several of these congregations in England, and they mushroomed by 1625.

Dissenters and non-conformists formed many what may be called splinter groups of worshippers known under many names and holding a variety of views. Some of them later helped populate such diverse churches as Congregationalists (Independents), Baptists, Quakers, Unitarians and Presbyterians. Even within them they often failed to see eye to eye with each other and only came together as a force at the rebellion. One indication of the level of support in Colyton is seen in some often given names such as Zacharia and Patience, to mention just two with obvious puritan connections

Such attitudes and desires were very much in existence in Colyton and, as far back as 1632, Diocesan records show that Henry Parsons and Francis Reede were prosecuted in the church courts. Their crime was for refusing to kneel at communion in direct challenge to Archbishop Laud's ruling demanding compliance in this matter by all. It is this type of action that served to harden and shape attitudes towards authority.

In 1641 there came a requirement upon everyone to take the Protestation Oath of national loyalty but twenty-six of our townsfolk refused with one saying 'he was not obstinately refusing but scrupulously forbearing'.

The same year saw the ejection of Thomas Collyns, vicar of Colyton, of High Church persuasion. He was replaced by the puritan John Wilkins, an appointment that did not suit those not sharing the non-conformist view. However, such were the strong feelings held against Collyns amongst some that he was treated most roughly, his home was plundered and finally he was forced into hiding.

During the other major event in the same century non-conformist and local allegiances were apparent during the Civil War. Colyton was first occupied by Royalist forces until July 1644 when Parliamentarians drove them out. Shortly afterwards some Colyton men went on to help defend the garrison of the staunchly puritan town of Lyme Regis during their siege in that year.

For many, life was of course unsettled and disturbed by all this and it was in these circumstances and atmosphere that a Baptist congregation in 1653 decided to build the Loughwood Meeting House at Kilmington★. It was in a position well chosen amidst dense woodland, half hidden by a hillside and was a place of safety in which they might worship in peace. It straddled the then county boundary so that the preacher and congregation might make their escape into either Devon or Dorset should officials surprise them. They built it well with stables and basic cooking facilities so that those who had journeyed a distance might spend days there amongst other like-minded souls.

Loughwood Meeting House

★   It stands today as a preserved example of one of the earliest non-conformist meeting houses. Now in the care of The National Trust it is a quiet and tranquil spot well worth a visit.

Early congregation lists number 220 with 17 from Colyton seeking an alternative place of worship. Whole families would make the journey, walking over the hills and along the lanes to reach it.

In 1662 the Act of Uniformity was introduced with the intention of bringing all those who had departed the official church back within it. This attempted religious settlement was far from successful or peaceful, although to a degree it may have had some measure of success in Colyton. There were many who seemed to be both occasional conformists and yet dissenters at other times. Perhaps who you were employed by influenced behaviour in this area and persuaded some to be churchgoers for the sake of appearance. Now, in the Colyton ministry tables were turned and Wilkins, as a dissenting minister, was aggressively turned out of his living in the town, to be replaced by the previously rejected Collyns. (John Clapp, a rebel, provided accommodation in 1678 for Edward, one of Wilkins' sons, who was a plateworker and preacher).

Later, in 1662, parish constables were offered the substantial sum of forty shillings to seize any dissenting minister found to be preaching. Most of these persecuted ministers elected to hold services in their homes or out in the open air to avoid detection. Frequently they were informed upon and their houses broken into, possessions taken and members of their congregation fined. A few years later, in 1664, the first Conventicle Act★ served to drive dissenting worshippers further underground and thus was the start of well-organised prayer meetings, being held in secret, throughout the valley.

In 1670 the second Conventicle Act ★★ was passed and increased persecution. This legislation required attendance on Sundays and holy days at both morning and evening services of all and every person inhabiting this realm and not having lawful reason to be absent. It is easy to understand how acts

★   This forbade all meetings in private houses or elsewhere of more than five persons (in addition to the household) for worship other than that prescribed by the Book of Common Prayer.
★★ This refers to the canons of 1640 introduced by Laud which included the requirement that all clerics, doctors, lawyers, schoolmasters and others were to take an oath that they approved of the discipline of the Church of England as containing all things necessary to salvation, that they would never seek to bring in popish doctrine, or ever 'consent to alter the government of this church by archbishops, bishops, deans and archdeacons, etc'. The oath produced a torrent of abuse, there being many at that time who favoured a Presbyterian form of church government, and became known as the 'etcetera oath'.

like these served only to harden the resolve of many. In 1670 the Colyton parish constables John Holwill, Thomas Clapp, Edward Bond, Thomas Parsons and Roger Satchell received a warrant from the Clerk of the Peace to seek out and take into custody John Bagwell, Henry Hooper and William Stocker for non-attendance. In due course they reported that these men could not be found but one is inclined to question how hard they searched as, later in the story, we see how those on both sides of the law found themselves united as Monmouth rebels.

Likewise Daniel Toupe, a mercer and tobacco cutter, was another to find himself in trouble. He, his wife Mary together with mercer William Lymbrey and his wife Grace were prosecuted and forced to take communion in Colyton Church. Such an action led Daniel to become a leading dissenter and yet another who would in time rebel. Actions like these now facing the community only served to harden opinions and help speed the development of a huge span of puritan influence spreading from Lyme Regis to Exeter. Being a market town, Colyton, with all the comings and goings, became a major centre and focal point of dissent.

Now had really come the time of worshiping in secret, leading to conventicles★ being held wherever was thought to be safe. It could be a home, a wooded glade or a secret building deep in a woodland area. It is not easy to imagine the covert needs that would find a group of men, women and even babes in arms gathering deep in woodland all united in one idea, namely, to defy their country's law in order to worship in the manner of their choosing, unconfined by the narrowness of the prayer book and rule of Bishops. A lookout was posted and, if warned in time, everyone could disappear into the trees and hide until danger passed.

One remarked 'it was difficult to remain undetected because, as you reached such an area, voices uplifted in psalm could be heard and one could not but wonder if anyone not in sympathy might hear and denounce them to authority'. All risked heavy fines or even imprisonment for this crime and such meetings were to remain illegal until the 1688 Toleration Act. The years 1684 – 1688 were the worst in the history of Baptist persecution with men and women imprisoned and harassed in many ways – it cost folk dear

---

★   A Conventicle was an illegal religious gathering esp in 17c. One not sanctioned by law and particularly attended by dissenters.

to follow their consciences.

By the end of the 1630's it had become clear that the body of Feoffees were open supporters of Puritanism, thus the potential for a clash between them and the Bishop of Exeter was considerable. Many members of Colyton parish refused to pay tithes** for years which resulted in church officers taking them to the Ecclesiastical Court.

One of the consequences of these most threatening times meant the office of Churchwarden was avoided by many. Occupying it was viewed as causing more trouble than it was worth and several who took it later asked to be relieved. Such unwillingness is hardly surprising when you understand that one of the duties was to record and report those not attending church to the justices, for prosecution at the Quarter Sessions. One, Francis Bagwell, a yeoman of reasonable means, sought to avoid it by stating 'I am already called upon to serve a neighbouring parish'. Upon investigation it was soon revealed that in fact he had not taken communion in Colyton or another church for eight years! This led him to be viewed by the authorities as a man whose opinions and actions should be watched.

By the 1680s this reluctance to serve the office of Churchwarden in Colyton had become a major issue reaching national level. The Bishop of Exeter felt just cause in appealing to the Lord Chancellor to take action and make Colyton a precedent to keep peace and order within the church. In particular the dissenting clerk and churchwarden, John Gould, refused to take the required oath and became the subject of disquiet amongst the loyal gentry and church officials. A most significant letter written by him referring to events fifty years earlier makes things quite clear:

> In Colyton there are twenty Ffeoffees who have the management of certain lands for repaire of the church and other pious uses of which number this John Gould is one. And in their Booke of accounts they have entered and agreed to an order, that if any of their Body being elected Churchwarden and prosecuted by the Ecclesiastical Court for refusing to take the Oath of Churchwarden, That person so prosecuted should have his fine paid out of publick stock. This order was entered in their said Booke about fifty yeares since and still stands recorded therein. And wee have reason to believe that tis observed by the present Ffeoffees for that we have not gotten one of that Body to take the oath of Churchwarden without a great deale of charge and trouble.

Clearly had the Chamber of Feoffees with its puritan leanings not existed, pressure on the inhabitants to comply with church directives would have

---

** Tenth part of produce as a local tax or rent based upon acreage and price of corn.

been even greater than it was.

The more I read of events and attitudes the more I came to feel sure that if any of the dissenting landowners or merchants were asked for their view on their religious and political stance it would have been their opinion that they simply wished to uphold simple protestantism in opposition to the growing fear of Catholicism.★★

The often violent and aggressive persecution upon them only served to strengthen convictions and as years went by it became inevitable that the opposition to the government and church could only grow. Many a strong independence of view had developed and, when pushed too far, it easily converted to out-and-out opposition to authority.

One writer has since referred to dissenters as true democrats given their belief that 'there was no man born marked of God above another; for none comes into the world with a saddle on his back, neither any booted and spurred to ride him'. Men genuinely believed that shopkeepers, artisans and farmers like themselves had as good a right to rule the land as the greatest lord in the kingdom. The majority of the rank and file that was eventually to form the rebel army possessed no great political thoughts save wanting to be ruled by parliament, not an absolute king. Whilst recognising the need for a social hierarchy they desired an elected seat of power occupied by merchants, gentlemen and lawyers, as parliament was meant to be. For many it was a continuity of Puritanism and republicanism of Commonwealth days, which gives this desire for a more level society.

Whilst this story is primarily about dissent and non-conformity, it must be acknowledged that there were, of course, other sections of Colyton's population who did not subscribe to the cause. Many a devout churchgoer was content to have their life ruled by its authority and did not share the fear of Papacy to the same degree.

There is much to suggest that a degree of support existed for the Royalist position, which would inevitably mean that there would be some spying and informing on others going on, making the guarding of tongues essential

★★ In general there was a fear of Catholicism both during Charles II's reign but more so in that of James II. More particularly, however, nonconformists objected to Erastianism, which held that in a state which proposes but one religion the civil authorities have the right and duty to exercise jurisdiction in all matters whether civil or ecclesiastical, and punish all offenders.

in some company. Within Colyton's community there were some whose persuasions changed at times due to circumstance, such as the opinion of their employer or influence of family.

It is most probable that preparations by dissident sections of Colyton's community had commenced much earlier in anticipation of events, which might require their active participation. The Feoffees' accounts show 'an armoury of swords and muskets was regularly maintained and a Muster Master was employed to keep barrels of gunpowder and boats for their transport at the ready'. One record shows that an additional and secret supply of arms was kept on their behalf by the Constable of Stoke Gabriel, being left on trust and available when requested. Alongside this are reports of injuries during local musket practice.★

Jane Hoare's husband, 'a tender father and most loving husband dyed at Coliton, being killed by a fellow musket that stood near him and broke that splinters pierced into his brain about 4 a clock and lived till 4 a clock at morning but never spake one word after he was hurt'. The tone of what we can read helps to support the suggestions of planning a rising being both serious and advanced amongst many.

There was increased cause for this unrest when James, Duke of York, who had converted to Catholicism and openly favoured those of that religious persuasion, succeeded Charles II his elder brother. As James II he was thought by many to be prepared to use unconstitutional means to establish an autocratic and un-parliamentary government, which would deprive the Protestant gentry of their dominating role in the country. The Whig Party, a descendent of the Parliamentary Party, became its champion. One of its leaders, the Earl of Shaftesbury and the Duke of Monmouth (Charles's bastard son), became the focus of this unrest until it sparked first into plotting and then actual rebellion.

Rebel Scytheman
(Paul Hockey)

★   In her book Pam Sharpe says 'we cannot know the full role of the Feoffees in raising men but it is possible to speculate that they interpreted their ancient role of "raising soldiers for the king" as giving them every justification in providing Monmouth with a good part of his army'.

JAMES SCOTT THE DUKE OF MONMOUTH

In this modern age, I am not at all sure how to try and describe a seventeenth century Duke who was in fact a bastard son of an English King, himself an exile after the Civil War. The boy, named James, was born in Rotterdam on April 9th 1649; this was the man who was to become Duke of Monmouth, potential heir to the English throne and eventual leader of the last rebellion on English soil. His mother was Lucy Walter, Welsh mistress of Charles, said to be a lady of easy virtue whose own succession of affairs was widely known. Some suggest this was an unfairly painted picture by those with an interest in helping disgrace and discredit any possible claim of her marriage to Charles.

James spent the early years on the Continent until his mother brought him to London in 1656 only to find themselves clapped in The Tower by Cromwell. They were expelled from London and took up residence in Paris where Lucy was to die. Resulting from this James was put into the care of his Grandmother, Queen Henrietta Marie, in Paris and renamed James Fitzroy. With her, he enjoyed a spoilt upbringing on the Continent until in 1662 (two years after the Restoration of Charles II), aged 13, his father brought him to London. Welcomed into Court circles and publicly acknowledging him as his son, the King made him Duke of Monmouth. Although still at a young age, he astounded everyone with his exceeding good looks, apparently almost to the point of beauty, enjoying his mother's sensuousness and father's good nature.

His father, Charles II, was one of the most popular monarchs but also one of the most lustful and licentious. It is uncertain how many mistresses he kept but was at least fifteen and by these various women Charles produced some fourteen offspring. His behaviour set the tone for the whole country, which was recovering from the Civil War and embarking upon a period of sexual freedom and self-indulgence.

He was most generous in creating Dukedoms for those who served him well and amongst them six were conferred on his own bastard sons – four

King Charles

Duke of Monmouth

Judge Jeffreys

exist to this day★. A courtier commented ' the King was father of his people' and in low voice 'at least a good many of them'. Monmouth was the most favoured son.

At the age of 14 the King secured for James, Duke of Monmouth, a marriage, in 1662, to twelve-year-old Lady Anne Scott, Countess of Buccleuch and heiress to a substantial estate. The marriage was not consummated for some years, so it was not until 1672 that they produced a son. Lady Anne cared deeply for her husband but, during the years that followed, was greatly neglected by him and his open pursuit of other women. His amours were numerous and the accompanying notoriety not surprisingly led to an unsuccessful union. He was always to claim this marriage was at too young an age and far from suitable.

By the age of seventeen, in 1666, James caused Samuel Pepys to note of him 'vicious and idle and fit for little'. His development revealed a weakness of character, low moral principles, little intelligence, easily swayed and a procrastinator. In particular it was this inability to be decisive that was to make him easily manipulated in the hands of politicians and plotters and create a divide between an indulgent father and wayward son.

Depending on the source, there are many and varied descriptions applied to the personality of The Duke of Monmouth but he was certainly an extrovert and given to acts of risk and foolishness, often involving both drink and women. Descriptions of him vary from being greatly charismatic to a vain and arrogant person. There is no doubt he was a handsome fellow, popular at court and elsewhere, but inclined to run somewhat wild, often the cause of embarrassment to his father.

Having said all that it must be noted that he had displayed a certain talent for soldiering and at the age of seventeen, perhaps to encourage him to modify his behaviour, the King made him Captain of the King's Horse. Two years later, in 1668, at the age of just 19, he was promoted to Captain General of the English land forces. Both John Churchill (later the Duke of Marlborough) and Percy Kirke soldiered alongside him and shared a brave and celebrated exploit at the siege of Maastricht in 1672, of these two we'll

---

★　The present Duke of Buccleuch is descended from the Duke of Monmouth; the first Duke of Grafton the son of Barbara Viliers, the Duke of Richmond was the son of the French mistress Louise de Kerouaille and the Duke of Albans was Nell Gwynn's son.

learn more later at Sedgemoor. (A further Axe Valley link provides local Colyton interest in as much as John Churchill was born at Ash House, Musbury.)

Successful soldiering followed for the Duke of Monmouth leading him, in 1677, to fight as a volunteer for the French against the Dutch. A year later, alliances had changed and he fought with the Dutch against the French, distinguishing himself at the siege of Mons and gaining considerable fighting and campaign experience. In 1679, having just turned 30, the King despatched him to Scotland to sort out the Scottish Covenanters where he led a campaign, successfully defeating them at the battle of Bothwell Bridge. However, in victory he was at great pains to ensure his forces did not run amok as was usual after a bloody battle. This was to gain him considerable respect in many quarters, particularly in the eyes of the London public and helped to establish wider support. Always a popular public figure, the London masses lined the streets and cheered when he returned from the wars. As one was heard to remark, 'he looks every inch a Prince but with the common touch' and it was this that would make people rise up behind him when the time was right.

His life at Court continued to be wayward with popularity amongst some but lack of respect from others. Elsewhere he had the ability to foster an image that soldiers would follow or workers would find approachable – never too much the gentleman.

Whether due to his own desires and ambitions or the encouragement of others he became embroiled in the political scheming of the day. Amongst his circle of friends were some ill chosen who saw the opportunity to press their own ambitions through his potential as heir to the throne.

Political activists of the day conspired, plotted and counter-plotted at every opportunity against King Charles and his Catholic brother, the Duke of York. Within these groups, whilst not directly but at least by association, the Duke of Monmouth was found connected. His supporters pressed their claim that his father, King Charles II, had in fact married Monmouth's mother, Lucy Walter, and was therefore the legitimate heir. In spite of having no formal heir and this intense pressure Charles refused to confirm this, and insisted it was his brother The Duke of York, a Catholic, who should succeed him. However, the political manoeuvrings between supporters of

Monmouth and those of his uncle, The Duke of York, angered the King, resulting in each of them being sent into exile in the hope of cooling things off.

In 1678 there came the Popish Plot which failed in its plans to assassinate the King, but a year later the Country Party achieved a majority in Parliament and commenced further pressure upon him. The strong and very real fear of Popery led this party to introduce The Exclusion Bill to ban a Catholic from taking the throne.

In the autumn of 1680, against the King's orders, and with falsely encouraged optimism, Monmouth returned to London when the Earl of Shaftesbury's second attempt at the Exclusion Bill would go before parliament. If passed, it would ensure the Duke of York (or any papist) was barred from succession or occupying any significant political position. In turn it was intended to bolster the chances of Monmouth becoming heir to the throne.

It was in this atmosphere, and despite it being guaranteed to stretch the King's patience to its limits, Monmouth set off on a Prince-like 'Progress'★ of the West Country during November 1680. This Progress took in several places in Somerset, Dorset and Devon where there were known to be members of the gentry strongly sympathetic. These included the nearby Estates of Edmund Prideaux at Forde Abbey, George Speake at White Lackington, John Sydenham at Brympton D'Evercy and the Strodes at Barrington Court near Taunton, Richard Duke at Otterton, William Courtenay at Exeter and Sir Walter Yonge at Colyton. By the time this visit ended there was a firm belief he would have the support of many Colyton and West Country families should he return to claim what they all saw as his right to the crown.

Here in Colyton he stayed at Sir Walter Yonge's mansion home, 'The Great House' which still stands proudly today behind stone walls on South Street. It was bound to have been a visit of great significance to the town, prompting stories and gossip for months to come. On his appearance in the Market Square, as elsewhere, scores turned out to see him and cheer, many coming in from miles around.

★   This was a tour designed to test his support in the West Country and bolster his following.

He presented a charm and manner that was extremely easy and friendly with just the right word for everyone, be they servant or gentry. He was tall, dark and very handsome with the common touch and people loved him. As elsewhere, he was greeted with great enthusiasm; people lined the streets and filled the Market Place for a sight of the one that many saw as a leader amidst cries of 'God bless King Charles and the Protestant Duke'.

Imagine for a moment the setting in the dining room within 'The Great House'. Darkly timbered walls, long table laid with silver, goblets of wine and food a plenty. Around it were seated well-attired gentlemen wearing rich brocades. Into their midst walked a fine and handsome gentleman, his face half shadowed by his long curled wig, the green and gold coat and breeches glimmering in the candlelight. Jewelled brooches adorned the neck, holding together a lace collar.

Such a sight would have taken the serving maid's breath away and she might later tell how she found herself quite speechless. He looked magnificent, better than any royal prince, and at close quarters guaranteed to overwhelm any lady with ease – apparently a most common reaction. Sir Walter's butler, known simply as 'Soundy', must have been equally impressed as he was later to have been 'seen in Monmouth's camp'.

A few hours later, well fed and wined, the meal came to an end and others arrived at the house. Their identity we might not know but all were soon set in deep and serious conversation of plotting and organisation. Plans for the future were being argued and discussed. Everyone understood that talk of this nature was treason and by necessity reserved for within secure walls. Equally, amongst ordinary people it had become even more essential to keep the growing possession of seditious pamphlets protected from prying and suspicious eyes.

Sir Walter Yonge's hosting of the Duke of Monmouth doubtless ensured a method of continuing contact being put in place whether through intermediaries or by other means. With the cloth trade centred on Antwerp the trading contacts through shipping into Lyme offered every chance for exchange of messages and information concerning events on the Continent. It is most likely that visiting sailors and merchants from Holland brought news and took every opportunity to encourage anti-papist feelings in the district. Heightened dissention amongst some of our own population must, in part, have been fuelled by visitors from the lowlands of Europe where, for years, there had existed very strong anti-Catholic feelings.

This visit being of such importance, it must have left a deep impression on everyone and was certain to determine the future actions of many. However, we must remember not all were for rebellion and some to the contrary supported their King whilst others just feared the start of another Civil War, the suffering of which was still in their memories.

Ever-present the whole time during research was the question of what motivated such a large number of our Colyton families to risk everything. Who, if anyone, was their leader and what part might Sir Walter Yonge have played in encouraging them to participate in what, after all, was treason?

As we've heard, the Yonges supported the Protestant cause so it is easy to believe that much of the eventual willingness of Colyton men to commit for the Duke was encouraged by them. The family held considerable influence and sway in Colyton and inevitably their attitudes and beliefs would have influenced many of the townsfolk. If ordinary Colyton families believed they had the full support, encouragement and backing of Sir Walter Yonge how did they later feel when it was discovered he had stayed in London and distanced himself from the uprising?

Surely, viewed in hindsight, if this were the case it would have been seen as letting the locals down, making it difficult for him to return to Colyton and take up residence again without incurring the wrath and hatred of those who felt betrayed and had lost everything. These honest and hard-working people would have men perish on the battlefield, fathers and sons hanged and others transported with estates confiscated and families made destitute in many cases. This surely would have left a feeling of hatred and bewilderment, indeed a desire for revenge, but no evidence to support this has emerged.

The Exclusion Bill was thrown out by the House of Lords but such was the trouble caused that this was to prove a further and most serious breakdown in the relationship between King and son, resulting in banishment to Holland once more. There could be no argument that if he were to remain in England his presence would only serve as a magnet for the forces of dissent.

All this time Holland was seething with both Scots and English exiles and malcontents either out of favour with the King, Cromwellian veterans or by association with failed plots. Here was a hotbed of sedition and planning often carried out in an atmosphere of poor security with careless talk frequently being picked up or sought out by spies of the King. To all that was going on the Dutch government chose to turn a blind eye. However, from here the possibilities for clandestine contact between East Devon communities and the Continent were continual.

Much of Monmouth's time was spent in the Hague where his relationship with William of Orange became closer. Strange, when one considers William himself had perhaps more than just a passing interest in the English throne, having married one of its heirs in the form of Mary, daughter of the Duke of York.

Back in England Charles was, at the time, playing a dangerous political game. Despite being in alliance with Holland he sought financial help from the King of France to free him from the restraints of the English Parliament. A closeness between William and Monmouth would be certain to damage these interests and after a while Charles expressed royal anger to William of Orange at what he saw as unreasonable behaviour, conspiracy and a threat to his throne. However, his own plotting with a Catholic country was guaranteed to increase animosity towards him in many quarters.

A short while later, despite knowing it would incur the King's displeasure, Monmouth slipped back to London, but his actions simply continued to incense the King for whom there would be no peace whilst he was around. His position as favoured son long since gone, his position and titles were gradually withdrawn, making him a social outcast.

In Spring 1683 occurred the infamous incident of the Rye House Plot when evidence fabricated by Titus Oates of a plot by the Catholics to murder Charles was exposed. Monmouth and other close associates were tainted by this and whilst conducting another 'Royal Progress' to Stafford he found himself arrested, albeit without foundation, for disturbing the peace, resulting in his being totally banned from Court. Such a progress of gallivanting about the country with an armed retinue presenting himself, as an heir in waiting would, in many eyes, have been seen as tantamount to rebellion. Wisely and without delay, together with his mistress, Lady

Henrietta Wentworth, he and others slipped away once more to Holland. From now on they would find themselves and their movements the source of even greater interest to royal spies regularly reporting back to the King.

PLOTTING IN EXILE

Eventually, on the death of Charles II on February 5th 1685 aged 55, the political pace hotted up. The throne was taken by his brother, The Duke of York, who became King James II. With the hatred and animosity he felt towards Monmouth both politically and intimately coupled with the threat he presented, the new King sought to see him totally cut off without a penny and no chance of his returning to English shores. Now the very real fear of many was the use of unconstitutional means to establish an autocratic and un-parliamentary government, which would deprive the Protestant gentry of its dominant role in the country.

In England, Protestants and anti-papists needed to be careful in the opinions they voiced and indeed where they voiced them. It was not impossible for a man to have enemies who would find an opportunity of reporting a dissenting position and view to the authorities. On the other side of the coin it must be said life within England for a Papist was not easy as they were barred from universities, Inns of Court and all public life – it certainly was restrictive to be a Catholic at that time. However, given the Catholic King this would probably change despite strong protestant opposition.

The Catholic Church, like many churches, was unable to tolerate any dissenting opinion. Huguenots were being persecuted for their religion in France and now a Papist King reigned in England, with a natural favour towards other Catholics; it was feared there would be fast increasing numbers of Papists in all sections of government.

Equally fearsome was the prospect of greater persecution of English Protestants and enforced papist beliefs within the army just as King Louis had done in France. However, this in all probability would have proved difficult because, after all, England was a Protestant country with few Catholics whereas France was Catholic with few Protestants.

Amongst those in exile and like minds in England it could now be seen as a very real possibility that a son born to King James would be raised as a Catholic heir to the throne. Within these groups they talked of the last King's natural son as rightful heir and that it was possible his illegitimacy could be disproved. A belief was held in some quarters that King Charles had married Monmouth's mother, meaning Monmouth would indeed have the rightful claim as heir to the throne of England. It is unlikely this was so and no proof was ever produced. With great consistency Charles had refused to acknowledge him as his rightful heir despite showing him great favour at court and giving him a position in society.

However, supported by many who held position and influence but, perhaps it has to be said, with their own agenda, it was their intention to see a direct challenge being mounted against the King by his nephew thus setting in chain a course destined to end in tragedy – plotting now was to become actual rebellion.

The plotters all combined to bring great powers of persuasion to bear in order to convince Monmouth that all he had to do was turn up, supporters would flock to him. They said sufficient arms to equip an army would be provided and the crown was his for the taking. Likewise large numbers from the King's forces, many of whom had served with him in earlier campaigns, would desert to him and the West Country squires were ready to rise up in support. In the event nothing could be further from the truth. In hindsight it is most apparent that Monmouth was surrounding himself with ill chosen companions.

However, reports at the time suggest he had become content to sit back and enjoy a quiet life in exile. Ideally he would probably have liked nothing more than to have returned to the social life of London and comforts of court instead of existing with limited funds. The reality was that any such chance was gone forever with King James who, being on good terms with Monmouth's estranged wife, could ensure her cooperation in this matter of cutting off access to any of her money.

In the Spring of 1685 Monmouth wrote from Holland to the Duke of Argyle's secretary, 'think of the improbabilities that lie in our way' and 'for my part I'd rather be thought of anything than a rash and inconsiderate man'. In this same letter he indicates that a Dutch garden may have appealed more than a military offensive – 'I am now so much in love with the retired life that I never like to be found of making a bustle in the world again'. Does this seem like a man our Colytonians and West Country bravehearts would choose to follow had they been party to such exchanges?

Between those in London and the exiles there was much confusion and mixed advice. Messages relayed with uncertain understanding by go-betweens creating doubts as to who was actually willing to support the plotters and how much money would be forthcoming to buy arms. In the end the chief backers in London refused to send funds as they began to believe the time may not be right and any attempt would be ill prepared, leading to failure. All this only served to increase Monmouth's reluctance. Nonetheless he was finally to succumb to the endless pressure but the level of his commitment became even more questionable as events unfolded.

Elsewhere everything was moving in earnest amongst the plotters with the Duke of Argyle, one of the main instigators of rebellion, finalising his plans to lead an invasion of Scotland whilst Monmouth was encouraged by the English Earl of Shaftesbury to lead in the south. Other principal participants were John Wildman, that professional plotter linked with the Rye House Plot, Robert Ferguson, a Scots preacher ousted from his living in a Kent Parish and an anarchist who would plot against any authority, Sir Thomas Armstrong (a long-time friend and mentor of Monmouth and described by one as a rake, duellist, libertine and lewd bully), together with others of whom, on close examination, intent, motives and character may seem questionable.

Time was running out and planning to mount an invasion to wrest the throne from his uncle became hasty to say the least. Finally it came down to Monmouth and friends deciding to pawn much of their possessions. His mistress, Lady Henrietta Wentworth, sold jewellery which raised about £1,000 whilst the Duke's silver plate a further £3,000. Eventually the sum of £8,733 was available towards a force of arms and men. Of this £5,300 was spent on the frigate, which, whilst well armed, was unlikely to be asked to fire a gun in anger. An exceedingly poor and ill judged investment when compared to the need to equip an army on landing. It had been expected that Colonel Wildman, an English plotter, would send more money towards supplies. He failed to do so, instead joined others in assuring Monmouth that, upon his arrival, sufficient arms would be waiting for him.

The date of departure was chosen to coincide with parliament being in session, which would, it was hoped, mean a delay in Royalist forces being organised as leading figures would be out of their counties and in London. However, this also meant many of Monmouth's own key supporters would also be in London and this was to make it easy for the authorities to detain or hinder them and thus neutralise their usefulness to the rebel forces.

Lyme had always represented a perfect place to land his invasion forces, as here they were sure to be met with a great welcome. The port was as well known as Colyton for dissent and was well placed to gain easy access to the important towns of Taunton, Bristol, Bath and the heart of his West Country support. All the places where it was believed people were primed and ready to give their all for his Godly cause.

The Duke's agent, Christopher Battiscombe, had made visits in the spring to provide the gentry and other leaders with notice of the imminent arrival of their 'upholder of the protestant religion'. Sir Walter Yonge was no doubt on that list and urged to meet Monmouth on his arrival. There is good reason to believe that by now the previously displayed enthusiasm and confidence of Yonge and the other gentry had become somewhat diminished. Rumours circulated in London indicating Monmouth's plans were no secret from the King and already military plans to put down any rebellion were advancing. If this were the case then Monmouth's supporters amongst the gentry would not sleep soundly in their beds at night for fear of apprehension. Key men in towns and villages in the southwest would also have become aware that vessels had left Holland with the Duke and his supporters on board and the time to stand up and be counted was fast approaching.

Monmouth's own diary stated 'we finally departed at 2am on Sunday morning 31st. May but it was extremes of wind and weather that delayed greatly our progress'.

Records of his ship's manifest listed four small field carriage guns, 1,500 foot soldier arms, 1,500 sets of body armour, 200 barrels of powder and miscellaneous supplies. He must have known this was barely enough to arm the numbers he expected to rally to his flag and doubtless must have been the cause of some disquiet but he put great faith in the assurances that more awaited his arrival.

It is certain the Colyton men expected to be joining a much more professionally armed and led army, as indeed would all the thousands of others who would leave their homes.

TALK OF REBELLION IN COLYTON

As winter turned to spring in early 1685, the first wild flowers appeared in the hedgerows. But all was far from calm and peaceful as, behind closed doors and in quiet corners, plotting deepened amongst many of Colyton's townsfolk. News had reached this town that the Duke of Monmouth, exiled in Holland, was even now putting together an expeditionary force – its aim to wrest the English crown from his Catholic uncle King James.

It was just five years since Colyton's own Sir Walter Yonge had entertained Monmouth at his home, The Great House, and given promises of his support. Doubtless that visit had encouraged many workers and tradesmen to do likewise in the hope of securing their religious freedom and right to worship as they pleased. Actually seeing Monmouth had surely got the townsfolk talking and served to set them into one camp or the other. Whilst his charm had clearly secured widespread support there was, from others, an opposition to any action for fear of starting another Civil War and causing further suffering. As we can imagine, the subject had been the cause of much debate and argument from time to time over the past few years.

Whilst being impossible to know, in detail, all of the 105 rebels, the story is fortunate in having one larger-than-life individual emerging from the crowds to encourage men to join him and be away to Lyme and the Duke's side without delay.

It is the yeoman farmer Roger Satchell who becomes a key figure in the unfolding events, as one of Monmouth's staunchest supporters in the valley. As we've already read he held positions of influence and power in the town, serving, amongst others, as a Parish Constable and Overseer of the Poor. He had worked hard to gather sufficient money to own property and land in both Colyton and Honiton. Some remarks attributed to him suggest he viewed himself as an important figure in the community.

Striving to be successful, Roger found other ways to be involved in trade, putting his earnings to use as a merchant cordwainer (shoe and boot making). It was not uncommon for someone successful to become the financier that helped a friend set up in business, thus establishing a further profitable interest. It is this he had probably done.

Peter Bagwell, who later became a rebel, was also a merchant cordwainer whilst Joseph Speed, another rebel, worked as shoemaker and was perhaps employed by Roger. Quite naturally many who became rebels were in competition in normal life albeit sometimes at different ends of the economic scale.

Roger was undoubtedly well known in the valley and was one to make both friends and enemies. During the early 1680's, he had aligned himself with recalcitrant churchwardens and been known to refuse cooperation with county justices. Labelled a Protestant hothead in 1682, there followed an attempt to frame him in a sexual scandal concerning his servant girl, Mary Pease, and an illegitimate child. It is the emergence of that story that allows us to discover Roger also had a male servant by the name of James Batten.

Of Roger some said he had a reputation as proud and haughty with pretensions above himself in rural life. Of course, much of this may well have been caused by jealousy at his success in bettering himself. Whilst looked up to by some, it is quite clear he occasionally found himself the subject of salacious talk; whether from envy or not is uncertain. If we had stood amongst neighbours gossiping we might have heard one of the wives talking of his womanising and saying '*I'm sure he's up to no good with that young lass from the dairy, I notice she's had the sulks recently and he's been around much more than usual*'. Her husband adding for good measure that '*he seems to have a remarkable insight to rumours concerning a possible rebellion and I do sometimes wonder if he may be organising open support for such a happening*'. Another that '*he moves around and mixes with all sort – buying horses, selling land and raising money but surely he has too much to lose unless there's more he does in secret. There's many a one I can think of that would like to do him down if he's not careful*'.

Around the town were many ale and cider houses – often just a front room in a cottage where folk would gather after a hard day's toil to slake their thirst. Apart from the Bear Inn the hostelry probably attracting the largest and most mixed gatherings was the old Red Lion Inn. Located, as it was then, alongside the Shambles in the area behind what is now Colyton's old hardware store.

Follow us as we enter through the creaking old door into a dingy candlelit room with straw to act as matting and soak up ale spilt on the flagstone floors. At the rickety old tables were drinkers perched precariously upon stools leaning towards each other in earnest talk. It was a popular gathering place after a hard day's work in the fields or local mill and the strong brew was sure to loosen tongues as evening wore on. Here for a while everyone, cloth worker, farmer, merchant and others were equal as gossip was exchanged and opinions aired. In smokey corners of this inn men sat amongst their chosen companions with jugs of ale washing down bread and cheese. Roger Satchell, whose anti-Papist views were as strong as anyone's and well known to most, drew some around him urging their support for what was to come. In time he emerged as leader of the Colyton rebels and was one of the first to join the Duke of Monmouth as soon as he had landed and was with him to the end.

Since James II had taken the throne at the turn of the year it had led to ever-increasing talk about the prospect of an uprising against him. Roger Satchell, as always, was for settling things once and for all with the King and looked to his 'protestant duke' to take up arms and overthrow the papist King. On this particular evening it caused tailor Richard Daniel to say *'oh, your cause is right enough but it's your choice of leader I'd quarrel with. From some quarters I hear his heart's not in it and never was. Competent soldier he may have been but it seems his power of leadership is questionable. He needs the gentry and men of authority to follow him and I don't believe they will be prepared to risk all they hold dear for a man who many see as little better than a rabble rouser'.*

'If not Monmouth then who?' piped up Zachary Drover at which point heads again turned as Nicholas Hoare the tanner joined in to say *'There's a man in Holland with unassailable right to succeed King James and his competence and suitability are unquestionable to my mind'.*

He went on to say how he'd heard many express the view that William of

Plotting in the Red Lion

Orange, married to King James's daughter, was an excellent soldier, capable ruler and staunchly Protestant. *'Now he's a man I'd be more likely to risk following and would caution you to think likewise'.* 'Here, here', spoke William Marthers *'that bastard of King Charles seems spoilt with delusions of grandeur and kingship beyond which it's said may be his ability to obtain'.*

Others proved a little more cautious in their talk – often warned by their wives *'to be careful in their way as 'tis possible thee have enemies who would just as soon report ye given the chance'.* It was becoming more and more wise to choose your audience with care, as much now being spoken were treasonable utterances.

The truth was that opinions were much divided and often simply expressed, for example, by John Clapp, a mercer in his fifties with ten children and much to lose. *'I see nothing but trouble and misery coming upon this kingdom and 'tis unsettling for trade.'*

'Aye we've heard so much of bloodshed overseas concerning religion that all we want is to be left in peace to pursue our business and keep our families fed', came from the lips of mason Richard Wilmott.

'I hear from the last visitors from Lyme that arrivals coming off ships, arriving into port, being questioned as to their intent and purpose so it seems the authorities are getting well aware about the rumours from Holland'. This unnerving observation from Francis Bagwell the sergeweaver began to make the future look more dangerous for everyone as clearly the authorities had their spies out so words needed to become more guarded.

Elsewhere, others of greater rank will have held their talk within the privacy of their homes, recognising the need to keep opinions closer to themselves. Different stories, rumours and reports reached people at different levels depending upon their position and nature of their business.

Around the supper tables of the gentry and yeomen elite, whose knowledge of politics and implication of certain actions were well understood, many questions were considered. There was a reluctance to voice the view that it may prove premature to stand up and be counted for one who many saw only as an adventurer and whose efforts were seen to carry the potential for failure.

Some more sophisticated debate included observations such as: *'Monmouth gained much acclaim when he beat the Scots and certainly showed himself the people's darling when he rode thought the streets of London. They cheered him like a king when he came through the West Country not five years since'.*

Stories were rife about seeing the emergence of Monmouth as a leader but dampened by feelings that it was only influenced by his availability and encouragement by his companions in exile. *'He may have fought well but from all accounts he's not a leader of men and changes like the weather. Whoring one day and lamenting his sins the next all the while keeping a strange mix of company with his lecherous friend Lord Grey and those hellfire preachers and plotters'.*

'One wonders why Dutch William lets him live and plot without interruption and what's his plan in all this. If King James has no son then William, through his marriage to his daughter Mary, is next in line for the English throne. Would he really be happy to support Monmouth to success instead of putting some difficulty in his path I ask? What a cunning plot it would make for William to stand by to let Monmouth invade and have some success. If summoned by James he'd have the organised army and fleet to send to England to save King James crown and thus secure to his wife and himself the English throne. Admittedly, Monmouth would have to die in battle or be executed to remove the people's popular champion lest they still preferred an English bastard to a Dutchman for ruler'.

The names of those 105 Colyton men who before long would be recorded as joining Monmouth, either at Lyme or shortly afterwards as they marched through Axminster, is most significant. There were 375 adult males in a population of 1,500 so well over a quarter of them followed Monmouth, which, for a small town, was quite remarkable. Over half were mature men well over thirty, three quarters were over twenty five and some over fifty. Here were men prepared to go off and fight and, if necessary, lay down their lives for religious freedom; to them their cause was just and demanded this commitment. Who went from each family would have depended on many circumstances, some, of course, not having the courage to rebel. Would it be the father, son, elder or younger brother? What difficult decisions they faced and how they would have sought the guidance of God to help them. Most would have wished only one family member to go but records surprisingly show there were six Bagwells (three later transported), three with the name of French (one transported) and seventeen families had two members listed as rebels.

Looking more closely at backgrounds, it became clear they were, in the main, skilled and professional people as borne out by their occupations. At the later trials, ninety were listed as yeomen but is generally accepted as inaccurate and done simply for speed of prosecution. As well as those we've heard of there was William Marther and James Pyes, both carpenters, tailors John Savage (hanged at Sherborne) and Richard Daniel. There was Richard Wilmott, a mason, and shoemaker Joseph Speed. One or two others seem quite well off, including husbandman Phillip Cox who had lands valued at £58 per annum.

The average age of those who joined Monmouth was forty, which might indicate how many of their views were handed down and related to the Civil War period. Most seem to have had at least moderate means but an exception was Joseph Speed, a shoemaker, who was 'somewhat encumbered in the world'. All shared firm and positive beliefs like that of John Sprake, later to say that 'no Christian ought to resist a lawful power; but the case being between popery and Protestantism, altered the matter'.

The impression gained is that there were no paupers as large numbers relied upon their own skills for a living. However, for someone like weaver William Clegg, aged 46, all his worldly possessions were valued at fifteen shillings at the time of his execution. The youngest known rebel was John Abrahams who was only fourteen when he left town with his father to join the rebellion. After Sedgemoor he must have stayed in hiding because everything indicates he did not return to Colyton until 1690 but had a son baptised in 1696.

A sad tale involves Joseph Restorick, whose life had become a misery in the months before joining Monmouth. He'd married his wife Mary in 1677 and had their first son Josiah late that year and a daughter named after her mother, in 1681. Two years later the daughter died but an even greater loss for Joseph was when parish records show he had a second son christened on 18th September 1684 and within days his wife died and was buried. After only six weeks the baby also joined his mother in the churchyard. This left Joseph to raise his eldest son by himself but the following spring this young lad was laid to rest on the 6th April, 1685. For one man to suffer such tragedy it is likely he felt nothing was left to lose when he went off to fight.

One thing is sure that, during the Spring of 1685, preparations for a rebellion or military action had taken place in Colyton as evidenced by increasing musket practice and occasional fatalities reported amongst those taking part.

MONMOUTH ARRIVES AT LYME

Come dawn of a summer's morning on Thursday the 11th June, the people of Lyme first spotted three ships that had appeared some way off shore. Their masts flew no colours but local seamen reckoned them to be of French or Dutch build. One was a 32-gun frigate later identified as The Helderenberg, the other two of considerably smaller size but nonetheless heightening the curiosity of all. Rumours and gossip fled round the small town all day and increasing numbers gathered on the cliff top waiting to see what would happen next.

However, it wasn't until close to sunset, at about eight o'clock that evening, that men in seven rowing boats headed towards the shore, to the west of the Cobb wall, to land their passengers on the pebble beach. By now there was an air of great expectation with many whispering the thoughts that this was indeed the Duke of Monmouth finally come to lead a rebellion and claim his rightful crown.

Altogether a party of 83 men had disembarked and gathered themselves upon the beach. Amongst them were those who would be officers and leaders together with some who possessed essential military experience. From this crowd emerged a tall, dark-haired and fine figure of a man most elegantly attired. Now it became clear it was indeed the Duke of Monmouth, looking absolutely resplendent in a bright suit of green topped by a hat decorated with bright feathers. He called for silence and knelt on the sand, waiting until the others followed, then in a strong voice, thanked God for their safe journey and asked for a blessing upon their enterprise. Rising up he drew his sword and he led his army up the cliff path towards the town; before him was carried a green banner of the Country Party bearing the legend 'fear nothing but God'.

By now, people flocked towards him, filling the air with their cheering and cries of 'Monmouth, Monmouth' and 'long live the Protestant Religion'. As always his charm showed clearly through, producing just the right word or touch for everyone as he passed them by. It was this great and immediate attraction he held that would ensure his ranks would quickly swell in the coming days.

Here, finally, was the man the townsfolk of Colyton had met and feted just five years previously and now believed he was to lead them along a path to victory, albeit with great uncertainty and unknown dangers. In a few hours news would travel to them demanding their commitment to the Protestant cause.

Some in Monmouth's party had a fine swashbuckling appearance, with muskets over a shoulder and braces of pistols tucked into a waist sash, as they set up positions in the town and set about listing recruits' names. Meanwhile, others had been set to guard the town approaches whilst more were busy on the shore supervising the unloading of field guns, horses and supplies. It was the early arriving recruits that were lucky enough to be issued with uniforms of sorts, arms and ammunition but by the time men from Colyton were to arrive much would already have been distributed.

There can be little doubt that the twelve days spent at sea put him completely out of touch with developments and vital intelligence of the King's preparations to meet his invasion. Warrants had been issued to detain the likes of Rolle, Strode, Prideaux, Yonge and many others, putting paid to the essential support from the gentry at a stroke. Maybe they were choosing not to come forward after all but without them many others would lack the confidence to join his rebellion thus greatly weakening the campaign.

Even at this early stage, it was already beginning to look a little uncertain and perhaps, in the view of some, unwise to continue. In fact this was just the start of a sequence of events that was to constantly undermine the likelihood of success and bring about such tragedy. Monmouth and the others had become too committed and there could be no turning back.

NEWS COMES TO COLYTON

From this moment on, news of his arrival was being carried far and wide by his supporters and enemies alike reaching across the valley to Colyton, Axminster and beyond, during nightfall.

Just imagine how, early next morning, a horseman galloped into the Market Square shouting out the news and causing a crowd to gather very quickly. His shouted news that *'Monmouth has come'* and *'God save the Protestant Duke'* brought men and women out from their cottage parlours and workshops.

News reaches Colyton

Many were quite stunned but great cheers rose from the lips of others. Once dismounted, men desperate to know more ushered him into the Red Lion and a jug of cider was put in his hand whilst being besieged to tell all he knew to those now pressing around him. *'It's as true as I stand here I tell thee no lies. He landed late last evening to a rapturous reception. Lyme people flocked to him and I'll tell you this, he'll have his army quicker than anyone could believe'.*

By lunchtime, men in from the fields and elsewhere filled the other inns and drinking houses with everyone desperate to hear and exchange the news. Now had come the moment of even greater and more urgent debate, discussion and argument. At home wives and families became anxious about the decisions their menfolk had yet to take and gathered outside cottage doors in huddles to give each other support and strength. Young Ruth emotionally said '*I know our Samuel is sure to go but I do pray Father won't go as well*'. In many a dissenting household the womenfolk were as firm in their support for action as their men but choices of who would go and who would remain were not easy for any of them.

On this very morning, in one weaving shed, the doors and windows were open as the sun beat down that day in June. The shirts already clinging to the backs of the men working the broad loom, a jug of cider in the corner to refresh themselves. In burst a lad, come running from the Market Place, out of breath and heart pumping but desperate to impart the news just learnt – '*the Duke of Monmouth has landed at Lyme and he's going to drive King James from the throne and bring back the Protestant religion*'. '*Down with Popery*' he cried without a thought as to who might hear these words of treason. '*Hush now, be silent a moment for not everyone shares our views and you'll earn a flogging at least if the wrong ears hear your voice*' said Matthew the supervisor.

Elsewhere the word was being spread with Doctor Nicholas Thompson's house girl, Elizabeth, rushing into her master's study shouting, '*He's come master Nicholas, the Duke of Monmouth has come, and already my John is saying he has to go join him without delay. What shall I do for I'm so afraid for us all?*'. Quietly, her master rose and taking her hand in his said, '*Go about your chores and occupy yourself a while for I must go and learn more of what you say. Fear not for your John as he supports a fine and just cause*'.

It was only a few evenings previous, amongst friends in for supper and wine, that he'd listened to many a view. They'd supped and talked well into the early hours but suddenly it seemed an eternity away. On that occasion one wiser merchant, filling his clay pipe with tobacco in front of Nicholas's fire, had voiced the view that '*any invasion seemed a ludicrous miscalculation, pointless and much too soon, as the King had not yet proved himself the villain as accused*'. Another saw Monmouth purely as an adventurer and would pray that he should fail miserably in his quest, despite widespread fears that King

James might become too influenced by his cousin Louis of France and seek to return England to Catholic rule. (In reality this was most unlikely given the great difference in religious makeup of populations.) His mind raced as it reviewed many of the other views so confidently expressed but no longer could he be sure from whose mouth they had come. Certainly one had wagered *'there's not one true born Englishman who loved popery any more than he might a Scot but there's surely not enough prepared to risk everything in rebellion'.*

Who was it that had said *'It's all very well leading men against authority but it's their necks that will find a noose around if all goes badly wrong. You mark my words there's great danger facing us now'.*

A whispered parting word in his ear returned to haunt him *'He gained a fine reputation fighting on the Continent and in Scotland but he is no real leader of armies for it's said his lack of decision shows through all too often'.*

Now, on this most dramatic of mornings, Nicholas found himself already passing the top of town from where he looked down to see large numbers gathered in the Market Place. At first glance it seemed all the apprentices and young men of the town must be there leaving the looms and fulling rooms idle. Changing direction a few strides further brought him to within hearing. Someone was stirring up a passion for supporting their Protestant Duke. He noticed, on the edge of the crowd, stood the Parish Constable doubtless charged with reporting the names of those reckless enough to utter treason in such public a fashion. Someone shouted for the Constable to arrest that man for his unlawful preaching of dissent and disturbing the peace. However, the Constable seemed to sense more would be against such action than for it so wisely held back.

John Freake, Bailiffe to the Feoffees, was nearby but kept quietly out of view for he knew, only too well, decisions were now called for that could no longer be postponed. Finally the time had come for dissenters and non-conformists from all quarters to stand up and be counted, amongst whom were many he counted as friends. As time went on he noticed a few quietly slip away, doubtless to put their packs together and whatever weapon they had and prepare to take leave of their families. Others remained in the Square quite willing to shout support for Monmouth's local followers but not yet finding the courage to join them.

Opinions in Colyton, as elsewhere, varied greatly, despite the area being so strongly Protestant and it has to be said there were many firmly against any thought of open rebellion for differing reasons. Outside the vicarage there was some loud talking being done. *''Tis a madness come upon us again and sure to split us apart'*, to which the reply, *'They fear for themselves, their families, the future of their country and their religion'*. Each would now be active in their attempts to persuade and influence friends and neighbours. *'What is wrong with a simple desire for justice and an end to persecution? Can you in all honesty blame them for taking up arms?'*, from the lips of another.

'Have we not had enough suffering in our lives these past years. It was hard enough surviving the fighting in our streets during that Civil War that split some of our families apart.' For many it had been a period of suffering as it wasn't long since the plague ravished the town, taking over 450 lives. *'Surely it's not too much to be left in peace and have no more suffering'*.

'We have some hellfire preachers that's for sure, more than capable of stirring up discontent and persuading some in ways that may not be prudent'.

'What of Sir Walter? He's missing from The Great House and is surely still in London where parliament still has session. Surely if he knew of the Duke's intention to land at Lyme he would be here in support. I know that Amos, like I, would dearly love to seek his advice and guidance. Were he here and if his support for the Duke has cooled he may at least be able to counter that enthusiastic rebel, Roger Satchell, and make some of our hotheads see sense.'

Events for some would now move quite fast and, by noon, the first to go and led by Roger Satchell, had set off across the valley. White-capped heads of women looked out from windows and watched in silent prayer as they departed. Close behind Roger was John Duce, a square-jawed muscular man with close-cropped hair and weather-beaten face, followed by a dozen others of mixed ages as they marched out of town clad in leather jerkins and carrying an assortment of simple weapons: scythes, pikes, staves and cudgels and the odd musket. One had two matchlock pistols looking so old they might offer a greater risk to the bearer than any target. Everywhere old weapons and armour, stored in barns and lofts, had the cobwebs brushed away now intent upon good use. A mile or so out of town two farmers on horseback galloped up to join them and onwards to Lyme they all went.

The following day the square still had people gathering. Word had come in that local members of the militia had been seen at crossroads throughout the valley, stopping and questioning people passing along the established tracks. It was clear their orders were to prevent more from reaching Lyme and joining the rebels now fast gathering. It was known that Royalist forces were also now approaching the town but, amidst all the comings and goings, men entered the Market Place from different directions, stopping on their way to hear what folk around them had to say:

'Mark Cox swears he saw some Militia not more than a mile away.'

'I'll wager the town will be occupied by Redcoats before this very day is out.'

'If only we could be left to just get on with our lives and worship how we wish none of this would be needed.'

'There's a madness in this King's authority when even our own Feoffees are in opposition' spoke James Battins.

William Greenaway, the worsted comber just turned twenty-one this year, strode determinedly to where a flat bed cart sat. Jumping up on it he declared to everyone in hearing: *'Two days have passed since Monmouth landed and many of our fellow men from around town have gone to Lyme. Roger Satchell led them from the first and I've word from him we too should join him and The Duke'*.

'There's never been a man more openly anti-papist' said yeoman Bartholomew Butter. *'I'm surprised he never got himself arrested. Is it really wise to follow that hothead?'*

William Marthers, who'd left his carpenter's workshop to listen to all that's said spoke quietly to his neighbour *'Six of the Bagwells have gone already – I saw them leave at dusk yesterday. I do honestly believe we've talked too much and now 'tis action that's demanded of us – indeed even my wife bids me go and God speed'*.

From the crowd the voice of soapboiler and husbandman Osmond Barrett called out *'Everyone knows Lyme is proper bursting with Monmouth followers, they've flocked to his banner from all over'*.

There were still cautious words to be heard when someone said *'Aye, but there's already talk the gentry are missing from Monmouth's ranks. Perhaps they don't feel he's the right leader. Maybe we should wait a while and see which way their fortunes go'.*

'Listen here' a woman's voice called out *' a farm can't prosper if our men go off to war. At times like this 'tis peace and patience what's needed now so think thee long and hard before you take a decision that's sure to change our lives forever'*

From his weaving shed had come twenty-one-year-old Argentine Rust who leapt up to join William on the cart. *'At times like this you may not always choose your leader but must follow he who appears and, indeed, your conscience. I charge you to remember that, when The Duke stayed at The Great House with Sir Walter Yonge not five years since, we all thought he looked every part a fine man and leader to most of us'.*

It was becoming hard for many in the crowd to follow all that was being said with emotions running high and everyone wanting to be heard.

With great conviction William Clegg said *'They're already stopping many crossing the valley and reaching The Duke. We should go before it gets too difficult to avoid the Militia patrols. I'll endure this persecution no longer – my conscience dictates I shall go and fight'.*

From the crowd someone shouts *'God save the Protestant religion!'* And another *'Every man was born free under God and so it should be for every Englishman'.*

'Let's seek an end to this and gain our freedom. We must have the right to live and worship how we choose'.

But not everyone in Colyton felt so certain of their action: *'I know it's said King James favours Rome but surely if he is persuaded to leave us alone to go about our business we should be satisfied. I'll not support anything that leads to more fighting'.*

All this ended abruptly when someone shouts that militia have been seen approaching the Chantry ford. William and Argentine, realising their danger, moved quickly to mingle with the crowd and slip away, one turning to the other hastily saying *'I'll be away now to take my goodbyes of family – there's no knowing where this will lead and when we'll return. I urge you do the same and we'll meet at Dare's Acre as the church strikes six. If there's too many of us it will pay to split ourselves into small groups to give more chance to evade being seen'.*

Within a very short while soldiers marched into the Market Place and lined up in front of The Shambles and their officer proceeded to read a Royalist proclamation offering a reward for Monmouth and punishment for any that join him. Displaying some courage one or two are heard to hiss and boo whilst others shake a few fists in their direction. Suddenly there's an atmosphere of fear and apprehension on the air as to what will happen next.

Three days on and as each hour passed more men had left and it became very obvious they were missing from their work or usual haunts. It was now up to the last ones to finally pluck up the courage and respond to the call. Tailor John Savage in persuasive tone is heard to urge *'If we don't support Monmouth and the others now we'll never be free of persecution'. 'I hear there's already a force of some 2000 or more formed up and ready to leave Lyme for Axminster any day now'*.

A few who fought for Cromwell were still just of an age to go but one old weaver, clearly past it, wished his son God speed with the words *'show them old Noll's soldiers may have grown old but they've bred sons like them to take their place'*. With some hesitation his son asked *'Say goodbye to Judith once more for me. Tell her I'll soon be back and to hold out for me'*. Placing an arm about his shoulder his father said *'Go off and do your duty lad and be assured I'll keep a kindly eye on your Judith. You need have no fears for her safety whilst you're gone'*.

It's now the last few, fighting with their conscience and seeking the great courage needed, who had yet to take the hard decision to go or stay. Everyone knew travel across the valley had become dangerous with the need to avoid the roaming royalist patrols posted everywhere, with the sole intention of restricting movement and stopping people joining up with the rebel army. Few of those deciding to join the rebellion could be aware of the risks of following this expedition or the real risks that they might bring charges of treason against the crown upon themselves and a terrible fate. They held the strongest belief that their cause was just and God was on their side. Thus it was their conscience dictated that they must go and fight for 'The Protestant Religion'.

As all these men set out from Colyton, they immediately faced danger of being stopped and apprehended although it became clear many Militia sympathised and didn't try to make things too difficult. Some in larger groups may have experienced the odd skirmish in order to pass along their way, whilst others travelled stealthily and unseen. Some were on horseback but many would have walked across fields and dusty tracks to reach Lyme. There were many an emotional goodbye of wives, sweethearts and families for none could be certain of the outcome and many thought of it as sheer folly.

Perhaps it is appropriate to stop and take a moment to acknowledge how it is quite impossible for any of us in the comfort of our twenty-first-century lives to have an understanding or clear picture of just what life was like almost four hundred years ago.

We have spoken of a small but prosperous town consisting of around 1,500 souls. In 1685 there were estimated to be some 430 males and the very fact that a quarter of them chose the path of rebellion needs considerable understanding. We have to remember there was hardly, if any, soldering skills amongst them nor would they have much idea of what war and battle would be like, apart from some tales and experiences handed down from those older men who may have fought in the Civil War, but that was over forty years before. The extremes of despair and unease over religious persecution did, in their view, place their simple, independent lives under severe threat. I feel it most reasonable to suggest there may well have been another quarter of the population who would have wished to have joined Monmouth but for one reason or another decided not to. Perhaps their employer was a conforming Anglican and it would risk too much to have gone.

Over the coming months not a single inhabitant of Colyton would remain unaffected by the events beginning to unfold. Colyton, like so many small towns, was a close-knit community where most people were acquainted with each other either through business, family or friendship. In fact few moved far away from the place of their birth.

Most likely, the ordinary people were in ignorance of the government's intelligence reports, which had given them every chance to begin organising their military plans to confront Monmouth when he had landed. Not only did the King know Monmouth was coming but by now had a good idea as to where he was heading. In London an Act of Attainder was passed condemning the rebel duke to death for high treason and a reward of £5,000 offered for his body dead or alive. Throughout the west, Militia forces were being put on alert and regiments of the regular army were setting their horses westward at a fast pace. Had our men known of this fast-changing scene, would they still have gone, one has to ask?

COLYTON MEN JOIN THE REBEL ARMY AT LYME

The idea of landing and forming a strong and effective army within days was greatly optimistic. Most of those expected to flock to the Duke's banner were untrained in the ways of soldiering and many would never have fired a weapon in anger let alone recognise the necessary disciplines an army requires. There was an immediate realisation of a lack of firepower and horses but the one thing of which there was no shortage were keen volunteers and within days the rebel force had grown rapidly. Men turned up all day long including those from Colyton who on arrival, as comes natural to us all, looked for familiar faces.

By the time Roger Satchell and his band approached Lyme, sentries of the rebel army had been posted and it was through their lines they were admitted to the town. Looking about them there seemed no tents for men to lie in but plenty of wagons filled, presumably, with the munitions of war; there were booths with things being sold such as hot meats fried over coals; fried fish, cold bacon, pork, bread, cheese and the like. Alongside were barrels of beer and cider on trestles and two fellows from Colyton were spotted haggling for food.

Following Roger's lead they joined queues of men waiting to be formally enlisted with their names taken and along with others made up into squads. Men like Roger would have been given a rank of authority and, whilst we can't be sure, it was probably as Sargeant, to lead his Company. At the Town Hall arms and ammunition were issued to them and guides then took them to outposts where officers introduced them in the use of muskets and spent the day under drillmasters receiving instruction. It wasn't long before some found themselves positioned behind hedges and banks to form a defensive position.

It was essential each man should be able to prepare their weapons in the correct sequence, to avoid injury or danger to others. Intensive arms drill consisted of the charging, priming and finally firing their muskets. They learnt that, if a soldier placed a double charge, forgot to prime or left the ramrod in the barrel, injury would result. Likewise, were any excess powder to be left on the firing pan it could explode in the user's face and it was only repeated practice that would serve to avoid such mishaps.

During rest periods, in between all this, Roger watched as more of his neighbours and others he recognised arrived in the field, for their training. All were keen to gather round him and find out what he knew. He could tell that their natural instincts meant they each wanted to stick together for mutual support as anxiety was in the air. Looking around he saw such a mixture of men, some in smocks, some in leather jerkins, some armed with billhooks, young men full of bravado but by far the most were sober citizens. He couldn't help but wonder how there could be arms for so many.

A number of new arrivals, not yet enlisted, were told by the officer to 'stand by and watch and learn some soldiering'. When a break came he called Roger over and instructed him to lead them down to the Town Hall. A short while later, down in the town the narrow streets of Lyme were thronged with a motley collection of men as never seen before. They came from all walks of life to form the foundation of this audacious army. There were weavers, carpenters, tailors, tinkers and candlestick makers. There were greybeards, a sprinkling of clerics, sober yeomen and young bloods from the towns. The sight of lace and silk was seen together with the occasional armour contrasting greatly with the more plain homespun and worsted. With battered straw hats and scythes over shoulders or staves in their hands here were good, honest, God-fearing men believing nothing but success and victory could possibly await them.

Passing an alehouse, Roger took the opportunity to enter the crowded room and edged his way to the serving counter where a jug of frothing beer was pushed before him. Taking slow sups he listened to various conversations taking place. Some were full of bravado clearly fired by alcohol whilst others displayed anxieties about the crops and fields left unattended. By the time he left, he felt most were desperate to set about their task to unseat the Popish King. Stepping back outside, he looked about himself realising he'd never felt so uncertain and anxious in his life. Back in Colyton he had land and money enough for a comfortable life. Not only that, folk looked up to him and his opinion was sought by many. Sure, he thought, there were some that had it in for him but jealousy can make a man behave that way.

Taking a last look about, his eye caught sight of a raised hand above the crowds and he just recognised the head of Isaac Abraham. But did his eyes deceive him or was that a young lad by his side? As they came closer his worst fears were confirmed, it was indeed Isaac's young son John, just fourteen. There was only time for a brief greeting as officers barked commands for men to line up and follow. *'I forbade him to come and his mother threatened all sorts but I'd not gone a mile past Colyford when he caught me up'* said Isaac. *'We argued more but if I was to continue here it seemed I had no choice but to have him by my side'. 'Tis my hope they'll insist he stay behind once we begin to march'.* Continuing shouts made further conversation or enquiry impossible as they parted company.

Realising he should get back up the hill, he, along with dozens more, made his way back up the lane all the while thinking how this was not a place for one so young as John. He was swiftly brought back to the moment on hearing a troop of horse ride up behind requiring them to step back into the hedge. Leading was a fine-looking man in purple riding coat and lace cravat. A periwig fell in silken curls upon his shoulder and this head was topped by a rakishly placed hat with white feather. The pale oval face, heavy lidded eyes and thick straight brows belonged to none other than Roger's Protestant Duke for whom he joined in the cheers. *'God send you triumph sir'* he called out. *'By God we'll give my uncle's army something to think on',* replied Monmouth. *'You can count on us Sir, we'll give our all for you and the cause',* replied another. It was to be just like this whenever Monmouth was seen looking every part a King, which is what most of his followers expected he would be.

On Roger's return the others all wanted to know how things were in the town and of the latest news. How many were now gathered? Had he seen such and such a person? had he seen the Duke?, when would they be marching out?, and so on. The most serious thing he'd learnt was that muskets and ammunition had run out and he felt that the truth should be spoken. *'We're already short of muskets and ammunition and I even heard some feared our success was becoming doubtful.'* Sensing the immediate unease this caused, Robert Bashleigh tried to introduce some reassurance, *'Don't let's be misled by all these makeshift implements'. They can be extremely effective –quite capable of taking limbs off if wielded with enough gusto. Our Duke may only have managed to bring enough flintlocks for a quarter of his army but we'll show them of what Devon men are made with or without firearms'.*

Realising the sense in this Roger added '*Our firepower is sure to increase as others join us on the march*'.

During the following days, simple and basic training was given with marching and drilling seen over the fields and hillsides surrounding Lyme. It was clear everything was to be done in haste but it was the lack of firepower that started to give Roger grave cause to worry. Recognising that most had no experience whatsoever in fighting, he was glad to see there were a few old Cromwellians around to give a lead to many a young man, which helped a little. In reality there were just enough days to knock this motley band into a marching army. Despite this, initial confidence grew as information emerged and spread how it was thought the King could only muster fewer than 4,000 men whilst Monmouth's camp believed they could enlist twice that number of volunteers. Once they left Lyme more would join with weapons and horses along the route.

Support of the gentry was crucial to their success but the truth was that none of them had yet appeared. Amongst the rank and file it didn't take long to wonder where these men were who had five years before feted Monmouth and made promises of their support. Indeed, of Colyton's Sir Walter Yonge there was still no sign or word, although it was later to emerge he had been forced to stay in London. One story suggests he may, in the event, have chosen to distance himself from the uprising. Clearly, in some quarters, there was substantial doubt as to whether Monmouth could deliver success. It must be said that gentlemen were indeed few in numbers, many having decided to keep their distance or, as later transpired, had already been taken into custody by the King's men. Knowing their importance, Monmouth continued to send messengers out to all corners asking why they waited and urging them to rise up now so others would surely follow. For the rebels' part, most would say they'd do just as good a job with or without the gentry and to get on with least delay.

By now some close to the leaders imagined that Monmouth himself was having some doubts about the campaign and to others that it appeared his heart just was not in the campaign. All had not gone smoothly, with a few setbacks taking place both in terms of skirmishes around Bridport and a dispute between two of his key officers ending in the death of one and return to ship of the other. In time these would be seen as adding to a catalogue of errors in judgement and leadership.

But for now time was pressing as by Sunday the 14th June there was certainty that forces of the Militia from Exeter and Somerset were heading towards them, so a quick departure was needed lest they be trapped in Lyme. On Monday the 15th June, the rebel army now numbering some 2,000 men, of whom by now upwards of at least seventy were from Colyton, and 300 horse set off towards Uplyme. The women and girls of Lyme threw flowers at the Duke and they lay scattered on the ground as his army followed (Some estimates suggest there were as many as 3,000 with him by this time.) Meanwhile, Lord Churchill was charged with leading the regular army, consisting of four regiments, west out of London to confront and destroy his old comrade in arms.

FROM LYME TO SEDGEMOOR

Their march brought them in sight of Axminster where, looking down from the high ground, the scouts had spotted the Devonshire Militia arriving at the outskirts of town and taking positions hidden in hedgerows. Confident in his numbers Monmouth advanced upon them rapidly forcing their quick withdrawal on seeing the rebel forces appear. Monmouth took possession of the town, set guards at its entrances but chose not to engage the enemy. It is clear from reports made at the time that the militia lacked heart, being somewhat weary from their own hasty march and probably with much sympathy for the rebels within their own ranks – indeed, some deserted to the rebels.

Camp was set up for the night and most felt bolstered by this initial success. Perhaps it was during that night men like fifty-year-old John Clapp, a father of ten children, and some other late decision takers from Colyton walked

Beginning the long march

into camp. The next day the army set off for Chard and Taunton on what was to be a long and wasted march. They were well used to the roads being dry and dusty during the month of June but now, swarming with soldiers and the hundreds of ordinary men from the fields, they became choking and uncomfortable in the extreme.

The lucky few travelled with sword and uniform of sorts whilst in the main they marched in homespun and everyday clothes, regimental colours fastened to their armbands, a sprig of greenery in their hats and scythes over their shoulders or staves in their hands. They'd bravely taken leave of wives, sweethearts and children but, by now, the realities of their mission brought with it natural anxieties. To keep spirits high Monmouth made sure he was well seen and when spotted, with feathered hat sat rakishly upon his wigged head, they'd raise a cheer. All along the route of their travel, ever increasing hordes of countrymen flocked to his ranks – Puritans who were angry at the king's religion, shopkeepers, blacksmiths and husbandmen, at this time none possessing any other thought but victory. None considered the risk of a horrible death and ruination for their families in the event of failure of this campaign. Few sought excitement, only justice for the cause and it was inevitable that, as time went on, they would become increasingly aware of the dangers.

From now on everyone back home in Colyton received only scant news of progress carried by the occasional traveller passing their way. Life in the town, over the next few weeks, continued as normal with shops opening, children going to school, church bells ringing and the weekly market held. Townsfolk talked amongst themselves but with a distance forming between those whose men had gone and those who'd stayed behind, for whatever reasons. Wives and sweethearts suffered real fear and anxiety with the uncertainty of it all, although at this time none could imagine the tragedy waiting to unfold.

I feel convinced that the Colyton rebels went off believing their cause was so just and numbers so great that this alone would bring them an almost bloodless victory. Men like husbandman Phillip Cox no doubt thinking the campaign would be over in a couple of weeks and he'd be home again tending the crops. At home in Colyton the father of one rebel son said '*they know they need success to breed success, but so far it seems there's only been scrappy and inconclusive skirmishes. They need a battle quickly and one they must be sure to win convincingly*'.

In the next few days the rebels passed through Chard, arriving at Taunton on the 18th June. Here, three days later, Monmouth was persuaded to be proclaimed King in the hope of finally attracting the Whig gentry from the west to join him. For many this sat uncomfortably and caused mixed reaction within his ranks but there was no going back. By now his army numbered some five to six thousand foot soldiers and over a thousand horse. A fine and proud sight they made marching out of town in a curving line as far as the eye could see and headed by the troop of cavalry. Ill equipped they may have been but there was proudness in their step from the belief held in their heart. The rest given to their tiring limbs had raised their spirits and many joined in heartily singing psalms and hymns led by black-dressed preachers, marching in their midst.

Yet to come was the problem and difficulties of arming and rationing such numbers. Increasingly it would be a necessity to raid farms and businesses for supplies, albeit with promissory notes of later reimbursement.

Unknown to Monmouth the Royalist forces under Lord Churchill were reinforcing fast with the weaker militia becoming strengthened by the arrival of the regular army. The rebels may have had the greater numbers but the quality and firepower building against them was infinitely superior and beginning to bear down upon them.

Cleverly, Churchill chose to have his forces dog their path, satisfied to engage only in minor skirmishes intending to disturb and unsettle his opponents. Much worse, and for many an innocent community, was the arrival of Colonel Percy Kirke's Tangier Regiment, renowned as being rough, brutal and corrupt. They'd been made that way by the brutal conflicts with wild tribes in Africa and were guaranteed to put fear into any man. Their job was to actively patrol the area seeking out intelligence, often employing violence as a means of persuasion. As word of this reached the rebels it began to cause concern and unnerve many.

As the days turned into weeks it became clear that confusion was forming within the ranks with men beginning to question why they were marching over the same routes. A feeling of dejection formed which caused some to slip away, especially as they hadn't expected to be absent so long and there was work to be done at home and businesses to be tended. Some doubtless found themselves tempted by the posters offering clemency if they deserted the rebel forces. Increasingly, those remaining became more puzzled and bewildered at the lack of positive and decisive leadership.

At this point many close to Monmouth became aware of an increasing sense of despondency coming upon their leader. Lacking news of the expected uprising in Cheshire only served to increase his indecision as each day passed. Meanwhile, there continued much talk amongst the rebels and a reassessment of purpose and chance of success – those drifting to their homes left with a feeling of grave foreboding. Harvest time grew nearer and thoughts of crops, work to be done and quiet home life must have affected many.

As the month progressed it became grey and rainy with an increasing cloud, both in the sky and within the minds, hanging over Colyton. Occasionally a rider returned carrying letters and news of the army's march but gradually everything became more puzzling and worrying as little real success was reported.

In Somerset the weather was turning equally bad and rain was making the going tough. There was constant calling for more men to put their weight behind the cannon that brought up the rear and were getting stuck fast at times. It was enough to break the stoutest of hearts and one Somerset man was heard to say to his neighbour *'I'm not far from home and think I shall go there tomorrow. King James's pardon looks more attractive than the defeat I now believe may await us. I'll not risk my neck any longer and suggest you might do the same'.*

A letter sent back to family might have read: *'the weather has turned bad, the rain lashed down from starless skies and the horses at the front churned up the road into a quagmire. Those of us marching behind had to pull our feet free at every step as we squelched through mud and fast became a most pathetic and weary sight. The faces all around me showed the dismay and exhaustion of men who had tramped back and forth across the county for no discernable purpose; frequently short of regular food or shelter. We'd had little opportunity to shave and wash so bearded faces are now common amongst us all; we struggle on in clothes that are constantly damp, mud spattered and ragged. Like others whose shoes had fallen apart I have bound my feet as best I can. You'd not believe what a contrast we are to the loyal band of men who left with spirits high and a trust in God just three weeks before'.*

Somewhere in these ranks Roger Satchell reflected on the recent events and how, in the main, he and his company had survived the occasional

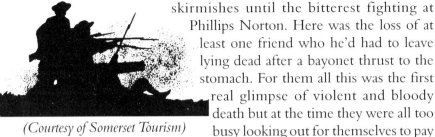

skirmishes until the bitterest fighting at Phillips Norton. Here was the loss of at least one friend who he'd had to leave lying dead after a bayonet thrust to the stomach. For them all this was the first real glimpse of violent and bloody death but at the time they were all too busy looking out for themselves to pay

(Courtesy of Somerset Tourism)

much regard. It was only now, during a brief period of rest, that the full impact of this experience hit him. He couldn't shake the memory of men dying, some maimed and crying out in pain, amidst a smell of cannon and gun smoke, which even now lingered in his nostrils. He knew his own musket fire had brought men down and for a while this thought sickened him.

There is little to be gained by telling in detail of the following two weeks' fruitless marching (which started at Lyme on 15th June) across Somerset. First to Bridgwater then Glastonbury, Shepton Mallet, towards Bristol, on to Bath, Frome, back to Shepton, across to Wells back to Bridgwater and finally Sedgemoor. Instead, let us follow Roger Satchell and discover how it now went so tragically wrong. Oh, how they would find themselves so badly used but the clock could not be turned back and face the consequences they must.

It is by now the 3rd July (19 days have passed) and Monmouth leads them into Bridgwater for the second time (previously on 21st June).

During the next day word reaches him that King James's troops, under the Lords Feversham and Churchill, have made camp at Westonzoyland. From Bridgwater's church tower he and his officers study their position through an eyeglass. By the afternoon of July 5th everything was coming to a head with Monmouth persuaded to launch an attack on the Royalist forces who were gradually closing in and reducing their options. Here follows two unattributed reports of the time.

'That night at eleven of the clock we set off under a cloudy sky that in turn obscured the moon and let it shine through. A mist hung over us as we began to near the drainage ditches we'd been warned it was necessary to cross. Everyone had been cautioned to the need for silence and it was an eerie march we made that night. Between midnight and

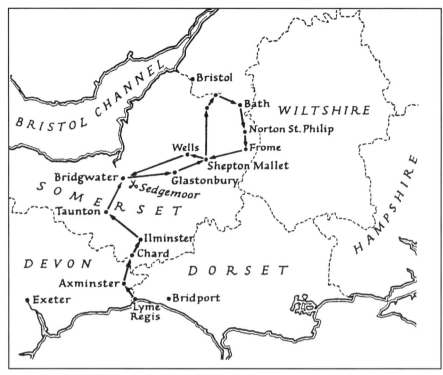

Monmouth's route from Lyme Regis to Sedgemoor

one o'clock on our final approach towards the Royalist camp all went terribly wrong. The area was riddled with these waterways and, in the view of many, more suited to an infantry attack but in the event Monmouth had chosen his horse regiments to lead us forward.'

It is now that we find reports of conflict, from simply an ill-chosen route which found their way over waterways to be impassable to tactical blunders and poor military leadership when it was to matter most.

'Mistakenly, or was it treachery within the ranks, a shot was fired and the enemy alerted. We were challenged by sentries and within minutes our advantage was lost as the camp came alive in their defence with drums beating and calls ' to arms, to arms'. You could see the figures moving in frantic activity and shortly an exchange of fire commenced. Within the hour superior firepower and discipline began to wreak havoc amongst our ranks and lines began to crumble. Our horse regiments blocked the path for we infantry to advance and our cannon lacked ammunition as it was bogged down

in the mud. Sedgemoor became a nightmare of blood and butchery. I, and all my fellow countrymen not skilled in the ways of battle, stood with useless but magnificent courage against the murderous charge of the Horse Guards. Our scythes and billhooks were of no avail against flashing swords and cannon fire.'

During the early hours towards dawn, the battle was at its height, Lord Churchill's fine tactical decisions produced strong and repeated Cavalry charges and the inevitable rout began. Men turned and ran, discarding weapons in recognising the reality of a lost cause. It is impossible to imagine the carnage that was inflicted by professional soldiers★, once they gained the advantage and the battle began to move their way. Rebel positions no longer held a line and as they ran this way and that, they were set upon by mounted soldiers with swords flashing, causing scythes to snap and rebels fall as they rode upon them, hacking to the right and left. The experience of professional warfare quite naturally demonstrating and finally proving an impossible might to beat.

The brave hearts from the towns and villages of Devon, Somerset and Dorset had given their all, but of course there were no soldiering skills amongst them to any degree. Once the cannon had been brought to bear to very great effect, it was followed by a combined cavalry attack on all sides, which closed in upon the rebels and forced them to break ranks and flee. Screams

---

★   Two military changes were the immediate reason for this. First, in 1685, England possessed for the first time a permanent professional army. With the single and brief exception of 1549, earlier rebellions had been met by improvised forces raised by great landowners, or by the local militia, forces seldom superior to the rebels in numbers, equipment, or training. In 1685 the Crown had at its disposal a standing regular army which, though small, was ready to be moved at once against the rebels. Secondly, just at the time when this standing army was being established, the effects of a revolution in military tactics, training, and equipment were being felt, which, for the first time since the appearance of the armoured knight centuries before, gave the professional soldier great superiority over the armed amateur.

and cries of agony filled the air, shrieks of the maimed, moaning of the dying, acridity of gunpowder and a sickening stench of blood – so much blood that in places it made the trodden grass slippery and caused horses and men to slip.

As daylight arrived the view of the fields of Sedgemoor revealed some 300 Royalist soldiers killed or wounded whilst a thousand or more rebels lay dead across the moor. The slaughter continued for another hour or so until exhaustion set in amongst the forces of the King and officers called for re-grouping. As our rebels crawled and crept away to find sanctuary and hide in ditches, cornfields and hedges, they left the field with their ears full of the cries and screams of the suffering of the wounded. Some of them were found alive by soldiers only to be butchered on the spot. In times of battle there never was, or ever will be, a time for quarter. Every man is for himself, which ends up with a desire to obey instinct and endeavour to be the one to survive.

Here we must imagine how Roger and the likes of John Bagwell and all of the others from Colyton found themselves in the midst of such an appalling scene. Experiencing the horrors of slaughter and blood lust, witnessing the carnage all around, but at the time unable to think of anything but survival. For these poor simple fellows, many of whom were more used to having a billhook in their hand and making good a hedge, the need to escape from the smell, screaming and groaning grew ever stronger.

Immediate retribution
(Courtesy of Somerset Tourism)

Let's follow the story that Walter Bagwell (who managed to stay at large) would tell. All that remained for him was the total urge to put as much distance between himself and this horror – no longer wanting or daring to be seen as a rebel. *'I knew there was clearly retribution now to be sought as men found hiding were dragged out, rounded up, pushed and beaten, prodded with bayonets*

*and some just lynched without ceremony from the nearest tree. Whilst I successfully hid
I saw one man badly wounded with a bullet through his shoulder and one in the belly
crawling on his hands and knees. A little later there passed close by, one man running,
forced along by two horsemen aiming hard blows about him. Even to my untrained eye
it was apparent that fresh-looking Loyalist regiments, who had not seen the height of
battle, had now arrived to round up any remaining rebels still alive'.*

The days and nights that followed would find him and others alone,
frightened and totally isolated from his comrades in arms.

IN THE AFTERMATH,
ON THE RUN & SEEKING SAFETY

It's impossible to say how many men from Colyton were killed or wounded on the battlefield at Sedgemoor on that fateful day in July. In the aftermath, many dragged themselves and friends away to hide and seek shelter from their pursuers. Fear drove them on as the victors were showing little quarter driving home a vicious defeat with some immediate hangings from the nearest trees, without trial or question. None could have foreseen such a terrible end to a cause in which their belief was total. Exhaustion and fear were now the driving force, for it was flee or die for them all. Many were just too tired or too weak from loss of blood to evade discovery and some would be easily betrayed by their fellow men now eager to find favour with the victors.

Consider for a moment the plight of some who had escaped the battle and now made their way across country unfamiliar to them. Once free and respectable members of the community

Exhausted in defeat

they are now traitors and outcasts on the run and in need of safe refuge. These were the most genuine of dissenters with trades and professions who had thought long and hard about the adventure upon which they embarked. None of the long discussions and debates with family and friends, over many months before their commitment to fight for their beliefs, could have prepared them for their fate. It was to be a fearful autumn and winter for those now on the run.

Where would they go? Heading for home would be the natural instinct to seek friends or relatives prepared to help, feed and warn of dangers. Everyone would know that giving sanctuary to a rebel involved great risk as the King's troops were out and about in search of them and danger of being given away was very real. Old timbered houses doubtless offered many hiding places or provision of a kind of sanctuary. For most of the fugitives it would be a long time before they could return to their homes without fear of capture. Many thought of the secret places known from childhood or little-known meeting places, perhaps like those of their conventicle, in which to seek sanctuary.

Over the days that now followed word reached Colyton and elsewhere of a great battle that had taken place at Western Moor. The news of the rebels' defeat with over a thousand dead, hundreds captured and many now on the run, caused the greatest of anxiety amongst the population. None of the families at that time knew what had become of their menfolk and started to fear the worst. Wives kept vigil to see who would risk returning home, whilst most quickly came to realise their men would have no choice but to stay in hiding. This was the start of a grim time for friends and relatives and was only to get worse as informers provided information to the King's forces now galloping into town in search of surviving rebels. Dragoons hunted, soldiers raped, rebels hid and widows wept whilst the authorities were hard at work.

Events in Axminster were a fine example where eight men were rounded up by local people who supported the King and taken to the gaol for which they were paid one pound for each rebel and five pence for the cord that bound them. The opportunity for some revenge or settling of old scores was considerable during this time and would have been experienced equally in Colyton.

Constables from each parish were ordered to produce a list of all those suspected of being involved in the rebellion, actually taken up arms, absent from their homes at the time or those who provided food or shelter in defeat. What a chance for some to even old scores, protect some for love or money or include the name of a rival in love or trade – a stroke of the pen would mark a man as loyal subject or traitor. Beside each name was a note of his crime such as 'levying war against the King', 'being in the horrid rebellion', 'following his colours', 'absent from home during the time of the rebellion', 'aiding and assisting James Scott', 'entertaining a rebel', 'for Monmouth', etc. Anyone absent from home during the past weeks for innocent reasons was to have a job to prove his innocence and was 'assumed' to have been involved until shown otherwise. Details were also included if whereabouts were not known such as 'not taken', 'not returned', at large', 'in prison' or 'dead'. Such was the hurry demanded of the Constables that they had no time to check their facts. Once on the list, a man dare not appear in his village, as his freedom would be taken. The records showed 76 such citizens were so listed by the Colyton Constable and 36 were names of men believed captured at Sedgemoor.

On the 11th July a John Bailes of Axminster was brought before Lyme magistrates accused as having a part in the rebellion. He chose to give the names of twelve men from Axminster and four from Colyton, one of whom was John Clapp, who he had seen in Monmouth's camp. This was just one example, which confirmed how there were treacherous acts of former rebels in the hope of saving themselves, gaining favour or obtaining a personal revenge.

The Constables' completed lists had to be submitted to the Grand Jury of each county to form the basis of prosecution at the Assizes. In fact, the lists were little more than useless due to their inaccuracy, as many men listed were actually not held in gaols and were either dead or in hiding.

All who chose the path of rebellion now risked a horrible death and ruination for their families. As fugitives they would be forced to live like cat and mouse with cold and hunger forcing many in the coming winter to forsake their hiding places in the country, for buildings closer to home – also closer to danger of prodding soldiers' swords in hay barns and the like. Offical proclamations made it clear that anyone giving sanctuary to a rebel would involve great risk as the King's troops were going to be out searching constantly through the countryside with the danger of being given away very real. There wasn't an old barn or ruined building that would offer any guarantee of safety or hiding place.

The impossibility of their position would have forced many of them to have sought a vessel bound for anywhere, from either the North Devon coast, or if they were lucky enough on the Dorset coast, but the dangers of that were, of course, enormous. It was a gamble to find a ship's captain who could be trusted not to give them away to authority.

Records and stories make it possible to pick up and develop some of the individual experiences of our townsmen.

Some did finally make it back to Colyton, scared, wet, weary and hungry, probably still in semi soldiers uniform of leather jerkin, sword belt and heavy boots – swords or pikes long since discarded or lost in the rout. Consider for a moment being one of Colyton's townsmen and picture his circumstance. He has travelled some 40 miles by walking and hiding, desperate to avoid being found and suffering a dreadful fate. The butchery and carnage of battle and massacre that followed had scarred his mind and all that was needed was to find a place of safety to rest weary mind and body.

This might well have been the story of the Colyton joiner Zachary Drover, aged 21, and separated from his father, Isaac, who he couldn't know to be alive or dead –

'Laying low till late that day I shivered and shook with cold and fear not daring to move on till darkness fell. How was I to escape from the tangle of soft banks, creeks, reed fringes and dykes without a map or guide? Hopefully my desperation would find me the strength just to get away from the angry sounds of drums, trumpets, firing and yelling – direction must matter not. Now for miles around I knew the search for escaping and hidden rebels would be in earnest.'

'I've no idea of the distance I covered that night forever having to duck into undergrowth at the slightest sound. It seemed hours before the noisy sounds of Sedgemoor were left behind. Eventually exhaustion forced me to take rest in an overgrown ditch and I pulled brambles, ivy and some branches close around me. As dawn came I awoke to the tapping of a nuthatch on a tree above my head and became aware of a rabbit scurrying away as I stretched a stiffened limb. What an unreal scene of peace compared to what I'd left!'

'Move on I must and some while later I hid up overlooking a small cottage and watched for signs of activity. Hunger and thirst were now to be reckoned with and food must be found but how was I to trust approaching anybody for fear of being pronounced a rebel and detained whilst soldiers were sent for. A common thief I would have to become and creep in to take what I might without announcing my presence. I made a cautious approach to be met with a smell of fresh-baked bread coming from the open door. Whilst chickens scratched around in the yard not bothered by my presence I felt someone must be close by and held back. Sure enough, a woman emerged and went across to the barn. As soon as she was out of sight I dived in to pick up a loaf and lump of cheese off the

table and ran back up the hill to some cover. For drink I'd surely find a brook to bathe my face and ease my throat.'

'The sun was rising as I spied a group of ten or more of my fellows on the hill to my left creeping down alongside a hedge behind this homestead. Thinking that if I should recognise them perhaps I should make haste to join them when all of a sudden from higher ground on the right was led a cavalry charge with their horses at full speed dashing into the midst of the group. Swords slashing side to side upon the helpless souls with not a weapon between them. I crawled ever deeper into my cover and prayed for them. I discovered later these were 'Kirkes Lambs' of the infamous Tangier Regiment – an ill chosen irony of name if ever there was one.'

For miles around, the search for escaping and hidden rebels continued in earnest. The days that followed were spent hiding in hedgerows and barns during the day to escape discovery by the lawless bands of marauding soldiers who steadily flocked over the whole West Country searching for rebels. These fugitives were hapless sights with clothes now torn and dirty, faces cut by brambles and streaked with blood – the buff jerkin stained black with peat and mud and a drawn haggard look upon the face.

We know Zachary made it safely home to Higher Paper Mill and during a search by soldiers he hid outside under a water wheel but his white shirtsleeve showed causing his discovery, and to be dragged roughly away for trial. One of the lucky ones, he was imprisoned in Ilchester but later to be pardoned and lived to the ripe old age of 71. Another, without certain identity, got back to his family and home in Bulls Court. Quietly taking the comforts of his wife and children he was alerted to the sound of approaching soldiers so rushed out into the garden and hid himself in a cabbage patch but had the tragic misfortune to be given away by his young son. One legend tells how he was seized, executed and quartered on the spot and his body parts pushed around the town in a wheelbarrow. There must be a huge question mark over such a tale and doubtless developed exaggeration over successive tellings so creating the myth.

John Clapp, the mercer and possibly Bailiffe to The Feoffees in 1680, owned a house on the main street with a double gable in front, known as the Bird Cage. He somehow made it back to Colyton and took to his bed. Some while later, awoken by noise of horses and commands in the street below, he leapt out of bed and up through a trap door in the ceiling of the outer passage to hide in the roof. Soldiers soon entered the room and noticed the bed was warm and realized its occupant could not have got far but after a brief search and failing to notice the trap door above gave up. John remained safe and free so that later he was to organise a petition on behalf of others to seek their freedom and, in this, obtained the support of Sir Walter Yonge.

A further punishment upon the West Country was the posting of regiments of the standing army. Colyton's high rebel profile soon brought problems for everyone as the

Safe for a moment

King's men became the scourge of the neighbourhood for some while. In October a party of Lord Cornbury's and Lord Churchill's troops of dragoons moved into Colyton. Initially there were some men captured and carted off to Exeter gaol for which there is an example of interesting entries in constables' accounts as: 'for carrying four rebels to ye gaol £2.10.0d' and another for 'carrying of six rebels in the sum of 6 shillings'. Surprisingly guides were needed on some occasions as roads were ill signposted: 'paid for men and horses to guide soldiers and others of His Majesty's messengers at several times £1-3-4d'.

Later contingents of the victorious army from Trelawney's, Kirke's and Dumbarton's Regiments remained in the town on and off for the next eight months until the King's amnesty in March 1686. They had borne the brunt of the rebel's firepower at Sedgemoor and suffered serious casualties so would not have been well disposed towards a town that supplied so many rebels.

Thus for the second time in less than half a century Colyton found itself under military occupation with all the accompanying discomforts, fears and sufferings as ill disciplined soldiers rode roughshod over this rebellious community. Stores were pillaged and unwanted attention forced on the womenfolk with wives ogled and daughters molested. Many had witnessed such behaviour during the Civil War years. Civilians' experience of soldiers found them little better than bandits and relations most strained. The townsfolk had to endure the typical brutish behaviour of heavy drinking and rough soldiers.

Those soldiers, on the other hand, felt they were occupying enemy country and not expected to behave anything like the disciplined soldier we know today. Whilst in occupation some amused themselves by breaking open the house of William Bird and carrying off bone lace to the value of £325. 17s. 9d, frightening his wife and children into the bargain and making them fear for their lives. After complaint and protest through the Constable, the Devon Magistrates were directed to go to Colyton, search out the offenders and satisfy Mr Bird.

As has been mentioned not everyone was for Monmouth and during this time the settling of old scores would almost certainly lead to the betrayal of some of the men folk. The very fact the town was made to suffer would not have sat well with many who were not dissenters.

One who never supported the dissenters passed the comment: *'save your sympathy, they were in arms against the King and took their chance. They cannot complain if they have to pay the price. They've brought such trouble down upon us all. There's crops not harvested, and looms stand silent, widows are reduced to begging and children are without fathers. I always said no good would come of this'.*

John Butter may have escaped official listings, as he remained at large. He may have risked coming back to Colyton after a short time so it's possible to visualise him showing clearly the signs of suffering with sunken cheeks through lack of food and feet wrapped in rags telling listeners *'The Lord turned his face from us. No matter where the King (referring to Monmouth) led us they shut their gates against us – even the common people began to scorn our cause'.* A sad and demoralised tale which continued: *''Twas being said he listened to poor council, which ended up with us tramping here and there getting tired and more hungry by the day. I've not known a roof or bed for these past weeks and I bin feeling sick unto death I tell thee'.*

Sir Walter Yonge came out of the rebellion unscathed, having stayed in London or as some have suggested 'detained' from returning to the West Country to join Monmouth. Having publicly hosted the Duke, he must have feared a charge of guilt by association but none was forthcoming. However, at the time he was building another house at Escot, near Ottery St Mary, and several of the workforce had left to join the rebel army. Two, who had the misfortune to be captured, were ordered by Judge Jeffreys to be hung outside the gates of Escot House – surely to be seen as a most clear personal and political warning to Sir Walter Yonge.

We should of course briefly include the fate of Monmouth who fled the scene of battle together with his closest officers only to be captured near Ringwood. Taken to London and imprisoned in the Tower, he sought an audience with his Uncle King James and begged for his life. His mistress Lady Henrietta Wentworth, and others sought to secure influence for leniency but failed miserably. In an attempt to save himself he claimed that the proclamation elevating him to King whilst in Taunton was the responsibility of others like Ferguson and not something of his choosing. How well that might be, but there is no refuting he allowed the event to happen thus being unable to claim no part in it.

On the morning of 15th July he penned a few lines or signed a note drawn up by others to the effect that 'I declare that the title of King was forced upon me and it was very much contrary to my opinion when I was Proclaimed. For the satisfaction of the world I do declare that the late King told me he was never married to my Mother. Having so declared I trust the King who is now will not let my children suffer on this account'. Later that day he approached the scaffold at Tower Hill with a restored courage and dignity, asking if the executioner's axe was sharp and passed him money to ensure a swift and efficient end. In the event it took several blows, much to the anger of the huge crowd watching.

Many of the Colyton rebels unfortunate enough to have been captured either on the field of battle or whilst on the run now found themselves in captivity. They, along with all the others, were squashed into gaols and buildings ill prepared or suited for the huge numbers involved. Conditions were quite dreadful, with wounded and injured men lacking in proper care and scared for the future. All were at the mercy of unscrupulous jailers prepared to help if you could pay or ignore you if, like most, you had lost everything. Rebels awaiting trail were kept in these most appalling conditions with smallpox and other diseases rife. Doctors and surgeons worked hard to treat wounds and tried to prevent the spread of infection. There was a real fear amongst the authorities that, if carried outside of the gaols, it would be spread amongst the nearby population. There was great confusion, as nowhere was designed to cope with so many prisoners at one time. Accurate administration was a problem, probably accounting for so many rebels being listed as yeoman for convenience of the clerks. Apart from town gaols, workhouses, churches and any other suitable buildings were used to keep the prisoners locked up.

Those Colyton men now incarcerated were spread widely over the three counties and not easily reached by friends or family even if it was known where they were detained.

Francis Bagwell found himself imprisoned at *Wells* along with John Butcher, Robert Cooke, James Pyes and John Woolmington. At *Bridgwater* were John Bagwell and his brother Peter along with Robert Teape, George Turner, Benjamin Whicker and his father John. They would all be sent for trial at Dorchester.

Poor William Clegg and Osmond Barratt were imprisoned at *Exeter* along with John Sprake. Conditions were so cramped and confused that it afforded opportunities for escape some succeeding by bribing their guards. Edward Barber and William Blackmore, both yeoman of Coyton, had been captured and imprisoned in the Exeter Workhouse. They were amongst a group whose escape was advertised in the London Gazette in September. Despite a reward for their capture, both survived and eventually returned to Colyton where each had a child baptised in the summer of 1688. Richard Daniel is listed as detained at Exeter but for some reason appeared for trial at Dorchester.

On the occasions when word had reached family and friends of where a loved one was held captive, they travelled in haste to appeal to whoever might listen for leniency or to secure their release. Certainly for those who had access to sufficient funds it was possible to buy freedom or kinder treatment.

Roger French and others almost certainly suffered the worst conditions, being incarcerated at *Ilchester Gaol* whose notoriety was legend. It was said to be so packed that it wasn't possible to lie down at night. Twenty-one-year-old Argentine Rust was wounded at Sedgemoor and taken here in chains, as was Robert Sands who had suffered two sabre cuts to the head during battle at Norton St Phillip. Roger Satchell had the misfortune to be captured at Chard by three troopers whilst making good his escape and also carried here. The confusion amongst the authorities is highlighted when you discover he was also presented at Exeter and listed as 'at large'. Twenty-two-year-old shoemaker John Skiffes and Nicholas Warren were later sent to Dorchester for their trial. Mason Richard Wilmott was released from here for trial at Wells.

Gaoled at *Dorchester* were John Heathfield, Nicholas Hoare, George Macey, William Marthers, John Moggridge, Joseph Restorick, John Savage and George Seaward. Peter Ticken found himself here as did John Truren, Edward Venn, Joseph Speed, Thomas Greenaway and his brother William, and John Knowles. Strangely John Starr was sent from here to Wells for his trial.

Taunton Gaol housed Percival Knowles, Humphrey Mitchell and George Robertson a broadweaver.

The experience of one John Coad, a carpenter of Stoford in Somerset, serves to highlight events taking place. He was wounded in the lung and hand at the battle at Norton St Phillip, kept at Ilchester and tried at Wells where he was to be hanged. In the confusion he took the opportunity to take the name of another prisoner summoned for transportation but not answering. He joined the group who marched under escort to Weymouth and then bound, by ship for Jamaica. Likewise the quick thinking of 47 year old John Restorick of Colyton provided him with the same advantage and ended up being listed as a John Standith and sent to Barbados under that name.

IMPRISONMENT, TRIAL AND SENTENCE

The notoriety of the infamous Lord Chief Justice Judge Baron George Jeffreys of Wem has gone down in history for his 'Bloody Assize'. Already a Privy Councillor aged forty-five, he had a notable career and a reputation for getting the right verdicts at many major trials. Indeed his rough courtroom behaviour had on occasions earned reprimands from the House of Commons, for his excessive zeal. In the seventeenth-century courts of law it was practice for Judges to take a much more active role alongside the prosecution than we experience today. Judges were hardly impartial and often just a useful tool to dispense the King's wishes at this time. If a witness was uncooperative Jeffreys would embark upon the most aggressive cross examination and haranguing to get to the truth, or what he chose to be the truth, quickly. At one time he thundered:

'Thou villain! methinks I see thee already with a halter about thy neck - thou impudent rebel'.

It helps to understand that, through the Judiciary, the Crown conveniently had a way of disposing of the unwanted or disruptive elements in the seventeenth century, by the death penalty. It was a most brutal age when there was no prison system available or places designed in which to serve a long-term sentence like today, so a man could easily be hanged or transported for crimes like burglary, robbery or rape. However, the plantation owners in the West Indies and America were always crying out for labour, and it would help them when transportation was the sentence pronounced. This provided positive support for the economy of the islands by increasing its workforce.

So, dispatched to the West Country by King James to try and punish the largest number of rebels in the shortest space of time, Jeffreys arrived at Winchester on the 25th August to commence the first cases. Accompanying him were four other judges: William Montague, Sir Cresswell Levinz, Sir Francis Wythens and Sir Robert Wright. There were few accused listed, so a notorious show trial of Dame Alice Lisle, accused of harbouring two rebels, was conducted. After this the party moved on to Salisbury where the only accused were those of 'seditious utterings and spreading false information'.

The next scheduled Assize was when things really began hotting up, with their arrival at Dorchester on 5th September. Here the really serious business of retribution started in the wood-panelled 'Oak Room' at The Antelope Hotel. Some three hundred awaited trial including twenty eight from Colyton and time was pressing. Events now unfolding were soon to be mirrored at Exeter, Wells and Taunton over the coming weeks. At every place were men from Colyton and would result in fourteen of its men hanged and twenty-two transported.

An unattributed lampoon of the time ran thus:

"The prisoners to plead to his Lordship did cry,
But still he made no answer, and thus did reply,
We'll hang you up first and then after we'll try!"

Those pleading guilty could find themselves suffering severe whipping or transportation, decided on the judge's whim, but at least their life was preserved. Some, if the family or friends could raise funds, bought their pardon, enabling them to slip quietly away. Pardon-mongers acted as go-betweens and not always honestly. Having given, in exchange for money, an assurance or agreement for a rebel's release or that a pardon was in place often, at the end of the day it failed to be forthcoming.

During this time, and quite improperly, clerks visited cells with the instruction to coerce prisoners to 'enter a plea of guilty that your life might be saved'. There is no doubt those insisting to plead 'not guilty' had the wrath of the court fall upon them. In one morning thirty were sentenced to be hanged, drawn and quartered and this was carried out within a couple of days, which left no time for appeal or pardon.

Jeffreys displayed great outbursts of ill temper from the bench for which some, in mitigation, offered the excuse as due to his being an extremely sick man with the suffering of acute pains from a kidney stone. Regardless of this, his brutality became legend and most feared. I am, however, firmly of the opinion that all taking place was preconceived and was directly at the instructions of a most revengeful King.

Such was the required speed of trial that thirty guilty verdicts were pronounced during the first morning in Dorchester and in total the town heard 300 sentenced to death, although in fact only 74 paid that final price. These unfortunates were sent to various locations to make public spectacles of their executions and strike fear into any who might still harbour seditious thoughts. Many sentenced to the whip would suffer this punishment through the streets of several towns or villages and in some cases it was ordered to be repeated during the coming year.

Colyton men ending up in Dorchester to face trial were John and Peter Bagwell, Phillip Cox, Richard Daniel, Roger French, John Facey, Thomas and William Greenaway, Richard Hall, John Heathfield, Nicholas Hoare, George Turner, Bernard Lowman, George Macey, William Marthers, John Moggridge, Joseph Restorick, Robert Sands, Roger Satchell, George Seaward, Joseph Speed, Peter Ticken, John Truen, Edward Venn, Nicholas Warren, Benjamin and John Whicker. For some stories can be pieced together –

Roger Satchell had been captured by three troopers near Chard and taken to Ilchester gaol. Now he was brought to Dorchester for his trial at which he met the inevitable sentence of death. He, along with others, was to be dispatched to Weymouth for execution but not before two friends had made an application for pardon or alternative punishment on his behalf. With great sadness, after considerable efforts, they had no alternative but come to him and tell him there was no hope, to which he calmly assured them 'my hope is in the Lord'.

Eventually whilst waiting his turn at the gallows he spent some time in prayer and meditation with a minister, the Rev. Robert Hallett, who asked what were his grounds for joining the rebellion. 'Had you been there and a Protestant I believe you would have joined too. But do not speak to me about that as I come here to die for my sins not my treason against the King, as you call it'.

A while later Roger pointed to the wood set aside to burn his bowels and said 'I do not care for that, what matters is what becomes of my body so that my soul shall be at rest'. Praying to himself for half an hour he finally urged some he knew 'never to yield to Popery'. Singing a psalm he allowed the noose to be placed around his neck and was soon turned off the ladder.

Roger was not the first to be executed that day so as he had waited his turn he was witness to others being dealt with. It is impossible to imagine or understand what faith and courage he and his fellow sufferers displayed on such an occasion. Bad enough to know he was to be hanged but to have to first see comrades dealt with in this barbaric manner seems incredible. Such was the religious fervour and fanaticism that in today's world we can only begin to understand by the willing sacrifice and martydom seen in, for example, the Middle East.

Of Roger it was later said that 'he was a bold spirited, courageous man of great reason, just and punctual in all his business and one that did much good among his neighbours'. His will, written in 1685, left considerable holdings of cash, accumulated through trading, which it appears, it was possible to distribute between family and friends and, by his wish, the purchase of bibles for the poor of Colyton and Honiton. Pamela Sharpe suggests 'he leaves an impression that his actions were of enduring importance in shaping elements of the community and local history'.

We must remember that the victims are not just ordinary partisans who joined a leader just because his drum beat loudly and without any consideration of the law. For many years they had fought for their religion feeling victims of an authority dismissive of their desires and had naturally come to a position when a stand had to be taken.

This is well illustrated by the words of Colyton's **Joseph Speed** on coming to his execution at Dorchester. On seeing a countryman and friend he called out – 'I am glad to see you here, because I am not known in these parts'. His friend in answer replied 'I am sorry to see you in this condition' to which Joseph said 'it is the best day I ever saw', adding ' I have not led a life so unchristian as many, having since the age of sixteen, had the checks of conscience upon me. I am not the least of sinners and cannot excuse myself. All men err, I have not been the least of sinners, therefore cannot excuse myself, but since my confinement I have received so great comfort, in some assurance of the Pardon of my Sins, that I can now say, I am willing to dye to be dissolved, and to be with Christ, and to say to Death where is thy sting, and to the Grave where is thy victory'.

Asked by some gruff soldiers if he was not sorry for the rebellion he said 'if you call it rebellion, I assure you I had no sinister ends in being concerned, for my whole design in taking up arms for the Duke of Monmouth was to fight for the Protestant religion which my conscience bade me to do, and which the said Duke declared for, and had I think a lawful Call and Warrant for so doing, and do not question that if I have committed any Sin in it, but that it is pardoned. Pray Mr Sheriff let me be troubled no farther in answering of questions, but give me leave to prepare myself in those few minutes I have left for another world, and go to my Jesus; who is ready to receive me'.

Then, calling to a friend who stood nearby, 'Dear friend you know I have wife and children who will find me wanting being somewhat encumbered in the world, let me desire you as a dying man to see that they be not abused, and as for my poor children, I hope the Father of Heaven will take care of them, and give them grace to be dutiful to their distressed Mother, and so with dying love to all my friends, when you see them, I take leave of you and them and all the world, desiring your Christian prayers for me to the last moment.' Then, repeating some passages of scripture and praying fervently for a quarter of an hour, said 'I thank God I have satisfaction; I am willing and ready to suffer shame for his name', and then the deed was done.

Having commended his wife and children to his friend and addressed the masses so powerfully the soldiers said they had never before been so taken with a dying man's speech. His courage and Christian resolution caused many violent men against the prisoners to repent of their tyranny towards them. Thus fell a fine and true man holding to his Protestant beliefs to the end.

The trial of **John Savage** and twenty-five-year-old cordwainer **Richard Hall** of Colyton took place on the 10th September and both were hanged at Sherborne five days later. In conversation one stated 'they valued most those that they saw no piety in and pittyed others that they saw not so well prepared' and 'the remembrance of our vanity may cause compassion towards such as were in such a condition, exhorting all to be serious and to consider their latter end, which deserved the greatest attention of mind, the way to dye comfortably being to prepare for it seriously, and if God should miraculously preserve us from this death now before our eyes; it should be the duty of us all to spend the remaining time, in such a manner as now when we see death just at the door'.

As the hour of execution came, their cheerfulness and comfort became much increased saying 'the will of God will be done, and he hath most certainly chosen for us which is best'. They submitted themselves to the executioner and later the quartering of their bodies.

Joseph Restorick was sent to Poole for his execution. As we've read his life had been most sad in the months before joining Monmouth and had little to look forward to.

What brave and courageous men we are looking back upon. How impossible it is to imagine the stresses, anxieties, anguish and torment they went through. A battle, imprisonment, a trial, and finally the realisation being faced that indeed your end is nigh. Not only fearful for themselves but for what was to become of their families. Arriving in the place of their execution, the waiting around whilst others were dealt with, watching their demise and finally to find the strength to face their turn.

It took just five days to complete all the proceedings in Dorchester after which plans were in place to depart for Exeter. According to papers found in Lyme's Town Hall there is evidence that Jeffreys broke his journey to visit the town on 11th September and was entertained by Mayor Gregory Alford and The Corporation. Listed are accounts for food, liquor and powder barrels for a firing of the town guns for entertaining my Lord Chief Justice and other judges. Whether Jeffreys was making a strong point as to who was now in charge in the county or simply to make arrangements for the reception and execution of twelve men being sent from Dorchester to be hanged the next day, is uncertain.

We do, however, know that gallows were erected upon the beach at the place of landing where it all had begun some 12 weeks before. Accompanying the Circuit party were executioner Jack Ketch aided by butcher Pascha Rose who arrived with military escort to hang the twelve men and deal with the quartering of their bodies. In this task they were aided in the tarring by a local expert to be known forever after as Tom Boilerman.

As elsewhere Sheriffs compiled lists and instructions for these arrangements which were as follows:

'Erect gallows, provide halters to hang them with, sufficient number of faggots to burn the bowels, a furnace or cauldron to boyle their heads and quarters, half a bushel of salt for each traitor and tarr together with a sufficient number of speares and poles upon which to fix their heads and quarters. Also to have ready a dray and wayne together with a guard of sufficient. An axe and cleaver for said quartering also to be provided'. Many a Parish Constable and Tythingman was instructed to 'take these parts and have them displayed on poles in public places where all shall see the price they pay.'

Quite understandably the Judges chose not to linger in Lyme to view the grizzly event so their carriages, surrounded by a cavalcade of soldiers, proceeded westwards. For us there is a particular interest at this point as Jeffreys didn't arrive in Exeter until Sunday 13th, having stopped and slept somewhere between Dorchester and Exeter.

Three authors★ have all mentioned the story of Jeffreys stopping for the night at the home of a gentleman when 'there was some disorder amongst the judge's servants and a pistol was fired'. It so enraged Jeffreys that the next morning on his departure he promised his host ' that not a man of all those parishes that were at that vicinitude, if found guilty, should escape'. The place of this lodging is thought by several to have been in Colyton and suggestions seem to strongly indicate it was at the home of Sir Walter Yonge at The Great House. What discomfort this would have caused to one known to be in sympathy with Monmouth and calculated to provide another strong warning of a quiet life being best advised. Were one to look at other possibilities then Colyton Cottage would be in the running for consideration as stories of such a stay have been suggested from time to time over the years but without any real evidence to support it.

So here it seems we have had staying in Colyton first the protagonist Monmouth, here to enlist support for his cause, and later the infamous Judge Jeffreys in an overt bid to demand conformity, no matter what position in the community a person might hold.

The following weeks would prove a mammoth task of organization and

---

★   Commented on in books: Judge Jeffreys by Woolrych in 1827, Duke of Monmouth by Roberts in 1844 and Parry's Bloody Assize in 1929. It is also mentioned in a publication by the MSS Commission. In all probability it originated from one original source and seems most likely to be true

stamina for Jeffreys and the four other judges accompanying him. The sheer number of rebels held, pending trial, made for an impossible task and fair trials were never really to be on the agenda as clearly there was no desiring of such by the King.

The gaols were full and the time at the Judge's disposal was too short to spend at each town where the Court would Session. Individual trials were out of the question and courtroom procedure had to be cut to a minimum. The task set was that it should take little more than a month to try some fourteen hundred men.

To give some idea of the implications of this, a quick count from records indicates this was the start when over a thousand would be tried in the following nine days, pronouncing sentence of execution upon 341 souls, transportation for hundreds with 33 fined and whipped. A few were pardoned whilst some just disappeared.

To sit in judgment and pass sentence on a hundred or more accused individuals in just one day was never to leave room for a realistic defense to be either offered or considered once again. Records leave no doubt that much which took place was totally preconceived. As a result most stood little chance of a fair hearing or justice. No one could dispute the fact that they had all been 'caught in arms' for Monmouth and little argument in law could be offered in defence of their action – it was indeed treason of which they were guilty, regardless of their beliefs.

Phrases of sentence became all to familiar such as 'That you be carried back again to the place from whence you came, and from thence be drawn upon a hurdle to the place of execution, where you shall be hanged up by your neck, but cut down alive, your entrails and privy members cut off your body and burnt in your sight, your head to be severed from your body and your body divided up into four parts, and disposed of at the King's pleasure. The Lord have mercy upon your soul'.

Alternatively there was a financial incentive for large numbers found guilty to be sentenced to transportation and in this the King was presented with the opportunity to bestow favours upon those close to him or to settle an obligation. These guilty rebels would be worth £10-£15 in the West Indies as slaves and thus he instructed groups of men to be 'given' or allocated to

An ACCOUNT

OF THE

PROCEEDINGS

AGAINST THE

REBELS

At an ASSIZE holden at

EXETER,

On the 14th of this Inftant *September*, 1685. where to the Number of 26 Perfons were Tried for *High-Treafon*, and found Guilty.

As alfo an Account of the feveral Perfons Names that were appointed to be Executed, and the places are to be Executed at.

SIR,

I *H*aving already given Account of the Pro. ceedings at *'Dorchefter*; I shall now proceed to to that at Exeter; where on the 14th of this Inftant, were Arrainged for *High-Treafon* the Perfons whofe names follow.

John Oliver	Thomas Broughton,
Henry Knight,	Peter Bird,
Abraham Hunt,	John Kamplin,
Chriftopher Cooper,	John Gofling,
Edmond Bovet,	John Sprake,
Samuel Pots,	William Clegg,
William Siller, Jun.	Walter Teape,
John Knowles,	James Cox,
John Follet,	Timothy Dunkin,
Elias Holman,	John Rofs,
William Parfons,	Thomas Connet,
Thomas Quintin,	

The Perfons above-named, being in Number, Twenty Three,were Indicted for High-Treason, and upon their Arraignment

deserving courtiers and the like.

Jeffreys was determined to leave a bloody scar on the West Country population and revelled in the sheer power in his hands to mete out the most appalling treatment to men who hitherto had been fine citizens, hard workers and (in their view) simply standing up for a freedom and liberty to worship in the way they wished.

Those who pleaded guilty needed no trial so pressure was brought to bear to gain as many such pleas for quick sentencing. Once condemned to death they had to be executed and the whole business of butchery was also lengthy, difficult, required a large number of tools and of course executioners.

The Exeter Assize was opened on the 14th with the clear warning 'that an unsuccessful plea of not guilty would be followed by an immediate execution'. There was a presentment roll of 494 names but in fact only 28 were actually available for trial. The first to appear were two bold men, John Foweracres (or Fouracres) of Honiton and Robert Drower (Drowser or Dower) of Axminster, who dared to plead not guilty. Both were quickly found guilty and, to encourage the others awaiting trial, Foweracres was sent to the hangman immediately and executed in the yard but for some reason Drower was reprieved just in time. Following this, four still pleaded not guilty of which two were executed the same day; 24 pleaded guilty and 10 sentenced to death. Of the rest, 5 were reprieved, 7 transported and 2 whipped. Of those hanged, drawn and quartered the Deputy Sheriff of Devon directed their various parts be sent to Honiton, Escot, Ottery, Axminster, Colyton, Crediton, Bideford, Barnstaple, Torrington, Tiverton, Plymouth, Totnes and Dartmouth for display.

Surprisingly only four Colyton men were set to appear here and they were George Farrant and Robert Hayman (pardoned and dismissed), William Clegg and John Sprake (Spragg or Sprague) hanged at Colyton and John Knowles (hanged at Honiton).

The local magistrates and people of Devon were sickened and shocked by the barbarity of the authorities and a storm of protest arose as the Judges left the city.

Travelling on to Taunton during the day of the 17th it was reported that

Jeffreys was in high spirits. Stopping for refreshment he was heard to laugh, shout, joke and swear in such a manner that many thought him drunk. The following day he faced the greatest number of prisoners with over 500 to deal with, of which 124 received the death penalty with various other decisions, of which we have heard, against the rest. The list of Colyton men included Osmond Barratt hanged at Ilchester, Humphrey Mitchell hanged at Nether Stowey and George Robertson transported to Jamaica.

At Wells, our men found themselves in the company of more than 500 prisoners from which 99 were sentenced to death. From the records they included Colyton's Francis Bagwell (transported to Nevis), John Butcher (due to be transported but escaped and was eventually pardoned in 1686), Robert Cooke (hanged at Norton St Phillip), James Pyes (had been wounded at Sedgemoor and hanged at Glastonbury), John Rowsell (lucky to be bound over and released) and Argentine Rust (wounded at Sedgemoor and transported to Jamaica).

HANGINGS IN COLYTON

John Sprake and William Clegg, both men of Colyton, were tried at Exeter on the 14th September and condemned to be hanged, drawn and quartered. Worse yet, such sentence was to be carried out in Colyton witnessed by friends, family and townsfolk. During the days they remained in gaol instructions were carried on ahead to the local Constable and Feoffees to prepare to receive them and carry out the judgement of the Assize Court. It was stipulated in the Feoffees Charter of Incorporation that 'should the King come this way or command otherwise, they are to provide twelve sturdy bowmen, duly armed, to attend him, or on any other occasion he may require'.

As a result of this, in Colyton a heavy air of depression and deep sadness was upon the whole of the town. By now they had learnt that five local families had already lost their men to the hangman's noose. Those slightly luckier, but they might have said not much so, were the twenty two families whose men now awaited their turn to be loaded into holds of ships bound for the West Indies. There was such grieving and outpourings of emotion taking place in so many homes and now those amongst them, of sympathetic mind, must show support for the wives and children of John and William.

It fell to their Bailiffe John Freake to organise the official reception, which, by interpretation of their charter, was their responsibility to oversee. Charged with keeping their weapons and armoury in good order was carpenter Isaac Drower who would normally have acted as sergeant of the hastily convened Kings Guard. As it was Isaac had followed Monmouth so Nathaniel Sweet, a craftsman of the blacksmithing fashion, was called upon to deputise in this most unfortunate of duties.

The fashion of 'boes and arroes' had been supplanted by the deadlier musket and the Feoffees, like good men of progress, had eschewed the older and obsolete weapon and procured a dozen firelocks of the most approved fashion, together with sundry swords. These were kept in the armoury closet in the corner of the Feoffees chamber. Thus from early morning, there were comings and goings from Church House with neither men relishing their duties of that day but no choice was to be had in the matter. The necessary guard of trusty men to keep order and see the execution performed must be provided.

On the streets men and women passed each other by with grim looks being exchanged between them that held a strong sympathy with the rebels. Many could scarce believe that such a dreaded tragedy would be re-enacted within the town despite the knowledge of it happening in Lyme just days earlier. The idea of a revengeful execution, after a mockery of a trial that had nothing to do with fairness of hearing, sat heavily upon most of the townsfolk.

Edward Bird, merchant of the town, walked through the town towards the Court House and found the streets almost deserted. Gathered at its door he found a number of persons including the constable and muster master and heard one say *'this is indeed the sorriest job ever to be encountered that's for sure. May the lord have mercy upon their souls, poor fellows that they be'*.

In front of the Court House and just a few yards up the Sidmouth Road stood three tall and flourishing elm trees presently in full foliage with spreading branches to cast shade around. Beneath these trees was a patch of greensward where children would play on a summer evening and parish merrymaking would take place. This was the chosen spot for the deed of execution to take place and Edward could see a group of observers watching as a man upon a ladder drove heavy fastenings into the tree.

The executioner having already arrived from Exeter, accompanied by the Sheriff's deputy to see them properly hanged, had shortly fixed his chains in preparation. He was a swarthy man with short black beard and slouched hat drawn over his brow to help conceal his identity. Now gradually a crowd began to gather there and around the Court House in Queens Square – not much work would be done that day, of that you can be sure.

Early that morning John and William had commenced their journey from Exeter along with a military escort. A little after noon word reached the town that the party had passed Stafford Cross, so old farmer Freake's cart, together with officials, set off up the road towards Colyton Hill to meet them. The two prisoners were not a pretty sight having been up since first light; they were dusty and tired from their journey. What a pitiful sight they made on entering the town and bound up in chains as they were. Their

A tragic day indeed

Dragoon guard was only too keen to transfer them into the charge of the Colyton authorities (the Feoffees Guard) and withdraw from the crowd to seek refreshment.

Both prisoners had requested the Vicar of the Parish, one William Salter, 'to provide his company and assistance in their spiritual preparations, suited to men in their circumstances'. In the event he prayed with them for some long while after which he asked them questions 'to give him and the world satisfaction that they were in prepared condition to be launched into Eternity, especially about the Doctrine of non-resistance'.

It was at this point that John Sprake elected to reply that 'I believe no Christian ought to resist a lawful power but the case being between Popery and Protestantism altered the matter; and the latter being in danger, I believe that it was lawful for me to do what I did, though God, in His providence, had thought fit to bring me to this place of execution'.

After reading a chapter out of the Corinthians and singing a Psalm suitable to the occasion he very vehemently and fervently recommended his soul to the all-wise God by prayer, for near half an hour, to the great satisfaction of all who heard him.

Then his wife and children did come to him weeping bitterly. He embraced them in turn saying 'weep not for me but weep for yourselves and for your sins as I have the satisfaction of being translated into a state of bliss and happiness where I can sin and sorrow no more. Wipe all your tears away and be diligent in the service of God to whose protection I commend you as He has promised to be a husband to the widow and father to the fatherless. I desire you fly to Him for security and preservation from the troubles that seemed to threaten this poor nation and I doubt not of our meeting in heaven at the last'.

A few feet away knelt William Clegg himself in great prayer and, asked by the vicar if he had words to pass, said 'John has said all that is necessary and they are my sentiments too' and then submitted himself to his own execution.

Now was the moment for their wives and children to be removed from their company into the arms of friends and relatives. As the final preparations were made both were helped up upon the cart which stood below the chains and stout rope suspended from either side of the tree which ended in a noose. The sheriff commanded the executioner to carry out his office and so placing the noose around their necks and cast them off the cart to swing. It was not unknown for the victims to utter words of prayer whilst their breath permitted it possible, and much to the distress of those attending this sad and tragic spectacle, some were heard from John's lips.

I have no wish to inflict upon the reader more than is necessary but do believe my shock and horror should be shared concerning the severity of punishment. The level of barbarity quite commonplace and accepted in England at this time is hard to believe and thankfully diminished fast in the following century. The manner of death for high treason was to be hanged, drawn and quartered and this execution involved suspending the victim with a noose around his neck until he was close to death, at which point he would be cut down and revived before being disembowelled and forced to witness the burning of his intestines and often his private parts in a fire. Finally he would be allowed to die before his head was being cut or hacked off his body and his arms and legs (the quarters) likewise removed.

Jeffrey's whole progress could be traced by the carnage left behind him. Almost every tower and steeple was set round with the heads of traitors and wherever a road divided a gibbet served for an index and there was hardly a hamlet to which one limb at least was not sent. Clear was the intention that those who survived should not lose sight of their departed friends nor the remembrance of their crime and punishment.

Upon Jeffreys' return to London on the 28th September 1685 such was the King's pleasure that he signified it by committing to his custody the Great Seal of England with the title of Lord Chancellor. Five days later His Majesty received all five judges at a public display to thank them all personally thus indicating once more the strength of his approval and support for all they had done in his name.

The following description of the beautiful West Country was recorded:

Some places have been left quite depopulated and nothing to be seen in them but for forsaken walls, unlucky gibbets and ghostly carcases. The trees laden almost as thick with quarters as leaves; the houses and steeples covered as close by heads as they might normally be by crows. Cauldrons hissed, carcasses boiled and tar sparkled. The stench was so great that many ways were not to be traveled whilst the horrors remained.

Just imagine travelling to Beer up Colyton Hill past Stafford Cross where there is displayed a head of one poor soul. Perhaps also at Shute Pillars and Pear Tree Corner might be the same. Maybe such horrors were seen at the river crossing by the Umborne or at Chantry Bridge.

It was to remain like this until the King journeyed to the West Country in the summer of 1686 when he finally ordered all the rotting parts taken down and buried.

Left for the crows

So many different stories abound surrounding the Assize and treatment of rebels. It is impossible to be totally confident of the accuracy of many due to an inevitable exaggeration amongst those with a hatred of the crown and still opponents, albeit now silent and inactive ones. Times of upheaval followed, and no sooner was some recovery taking place and accounts written down, that William of Orange arrived at Brixham and historians had another momentous event on which to focus their attention, follow and record.

SENTENCED TO BE TRANSPORTED

Other than hanging a very large number would be sentenced to transportation for service in the colonies and in this respect the King had special instructions for their disposal. By sending them to the islands, as opposed to New England or New Jersey, where the population would have been more kindly disposed towards them, it guaranteed maximum misery and punishment. The rebel prisoners would discover a climate very much unsuited to Europeans and a miserable existence which would fully equal that of Negro slaves working the plantations.

Many courtiers close to the King became aware of an opportunity to share in the potential profits this offered and lobbied the King for consideration. Those in his majesty's favour or due payment for services to the crown were 'given' considerable numbers of prisoners. In exchange they had to enter an agreement to arrange their carriage to the colonies and to ensure they were kept there for ten years before being freed. There were speculative profits to be gained from trading these convicts. The prisoners were to be placed into their custody within a couple of weeks thus relieving the crown of the cost and trouble of incarceration.

Subsequently Secretary of State, Lord Sutherland wrote, on behalf of the King, to instruct Jeffreys:

> His Majesty commands me also to acquaint you that of such persons who you shall think qualified for transportation, He intends 200 to the Governor of Jamaica Sir Phillip Howard, 200 to Sir Richard White, and 100 each to Sir William Booth, Sir James Kendall, Jerome Nepho, Sir William Stapleton, and Sir Christpher Musgrave and a merchant whose name I do not yet know. His Majesty would have your Lordship accordingly give Order for delivering such number to the said persons respectively, or to such as they shall appoint to receive them.

Thus it was that one thousand men were simply to be given away as 'rewards' or 'gifts' to be sold into slavery. For the convicts, they faced ten years before those lucky enough to survive would be free to make their way home or choose to establish a new life for themselves on the islands.

Jeffreys was clearly unhappy about these arrangements and argued that it would put money in the pocket of people who had played no part in their capture or borne no costs of putting down the rebellion. Such was his feelings on the subject that on the 19th September he wrote:

> 'I received your Majesty's commands by my Lord Sutherland about the rebels your Majesty designs for transportation, but I beseech your Majesty that I may inform you that each prisoner will be worth £10 if not £15 a piece, and that if your Majesty orders them as you have already designed, persons that have not suffered in your service will run away with the booty and I am certain that your Majesty will be continually perplexed with petitions for recompense for sufferers as well as rewards for servants.

Despite this, the King's instructions were adhered to which leads us to follow those Colyton men 'gifted', according to State Papers in The Public Record Office, to Jerome Nepho, elderly private secretary to the Queen when she was Duchess of York.

Warrant for Delivery of Rebel Convicts to Mr Nepho

Whereas the several persons whose names are contained in a schedule hereunto annexed remain now in your custody being attained for high treason for leaving war against his sacred majesty under the late Duke of Monmouth, before me and others of his majesty's justices of Oyer and Terminer for this Western Circuit; And whereas his majesty has been pleased to signify to me, his royal pleasure of his gratious intentions to extend his mercy to the said persons, and to pardon them their lives upon condition of transportation into some of his majesties plantations beyond the sea and for that purpose the said persons should be delivered to Jerome Nepho or order, he having already pursuant to his majesties commands entered into a recognizance for their safe and speedy transportation into his said majesties beyond the seas according to his royal direction, and is obliged to dischargeyou and all your officers & ministers from further trouble and the country from further charge, relating to the said persons within ten days after the date of these presents and upon such other conditions as his majesty has required. These are therefore in his majesty's name to will and require you forthwith upon sight hereof to deliver unto the Jerome Nepho or his order the said several persons in the said schedule named, in order to their transportation as aforesaid, and you are hereby directed to take a receipt from the person or persons to whom you shall deliver the said prisoners pursuant to this order of the receipt of them, and for so doing shall be your warrant. Given under my hand and seal this present 25th. Day of September in the first year of the reign of our sovereign Lord King James 1685

Nepho was now required to make arrangements and pay for their transportation across the Atlantic at probably less than £5 a head and then have an agent in the colonies sell them as slaves to new masters at £10–15 each. In the event Nepho, either through ignorance or perhaps being of insufficient means to bear this cost, entered into a contract to sell them to a pardon-monger and 'needy papist' named George Penne. This was a perfectly legal and normal transaction but by doing so he would have received only a small fraction of their worth. Late in September, Penne contracted for James May, captain of 'The Betty', to transport them as freight out of Weymouth to Barbados.

A total of 80 convicts and a servant woman were loaded onto 'The Betty', which set sail for Barbados on November 25th at the start of a dreadful journey and test of endurance across the Atlantic. The fifteen Colyton men on this voyage were Peter Bagwell, Phillip Cox, Richard Daniell, John Facey, William Greenaway, John Heathfield, Bernard Lowman, William Marthers, John Moggridge, Robert Sandy, Peter Ticken, John Truren, Edward Venn and (for whatever the good fortune to suffer together) were John Whicker and his son Benjamin.

In place was a most careful and detailed system to ensure the instructions for transportation took place correctly with receipts being required at various stages of their movement. From the first moment when the prisoners were handed over by the military to the first recipient a receipt was needed. Later certificates were required from and issued by ships' captains at departure from England and statements sworn on arrival at their destination. This extended to the island governor being required to witness the satisfactory conclusion in this matter. Later assessments indicate only around 500 may have actually been embarked for shipping so one has to assume great numbers must have escaped or gained pardons.

RECEIPT OF PRISONERS BOUND FOR BARBADOS

Received according to his majesties directions from
ye Lord Chief Justice with a schedule thereunto
annexed on one hundred persons attained of high
treason which are by Jerome Nepho to be transported
into some of his majesties plantations in America
according to a condition of a recognizance entered
into by me for that purpose.
In witness wherof I have hereunto put my hand this
six and twentieth day of September in the first year
of his majesties reigne 1685
                    Signed: George Penne and Charles White
                    Witnessed: Robert Hyde and Samual Gee

Even for ordinary passengers such a journey would be an arduous and dangerous venture, coping with five to eight weeks in a cramped vessel. Threats from pirates or unfriendly navies were a real danger whilst the perils of wind and high seas would test anyone. The prospect of seasickness would have filled most ordinary fare-paying passengers with foreboding but for the rebels their plight is unimaginable.

One story recounted tells of 'being locked in a dark hold with no light or air, the hatchways constantly watched by sentries armed with blunderbuss or heavy cudgels. An inadequate bowl was provided for our wastes, which was to guarantee there would be outbreaks of fever, smallpox, plague or similar. Around me the hold was an awful prison full of the crying and dying with little chance of sleep for any of us'. None were allowed on deck for air or exercise so for rebels Phillip Cox and Edward Venn death may have come as relief, when they died at sea on December 19th and were slipped overboard with little or no ceremony. Other rebels would perish in this way before the ship would make landfall of Barbados. Whilst living conditions were indescribable, their poor diet consisted of coarse biscuit and fetid water. Under anything resembling normal living conditions, each man would have been able to consume the ration being provided for five.

Finally after their ordeal and weeks of suffering they berthed in Barbados where the receiving agents for Penne's cargo, Charles Thomas & Co., were waiting for them. The following receipt confirms this took place on 8th

January 1686 but, of course, fails to mention how considerable was their loss of weight which presented an extremely sorry sight on arrival.

BILL OF MORTALITY DURING THE VOYAGE

The bill of mortality of the said rebels that died since they were on board and were thrown over board out of the said ship are these:

December sixteenth Thomas Venner, seventeenth William Guppy, eighteenth John Willis, nineteenth Edward Venn,the same day Phillip Cox, one and twentieth Robert Vawter, five and twentieth William Greenway, January the first Peter Bird, as witnessed by the commander and officers of the said ship this eighth day of Januray 1686.

Signed: John May (capt), John Penner, John Maddison,
        Gabriel Whithorn, Malcum Fraser.

Charles Thomas & Co arranged immediate sales, to plantation owners or others, some of whom were disposed of in batches but not usually exceeding a dozen. Some 'new owners' were purely speculative buyers who might choose to fatten them, just as you would with cattle, before selling them again in twos and threes to the planters who would make the final payment and for whom the prisoners became wholly slaves of their new masters. At this point these final owners were obliged to certify the number of prisoners handed over and each was then required to send an invoice of transfer giving names and destinations. In so doing these masters were also in fact entering an undertaking to ensure the convicts remained in captivity for the term of sentence, pronounced all those weeks ago in England.

If we may take the liberty once more to put words into the mouth of Peter Bagwell:

'Once the 'Betty' had berthed all of us were dragged up onto the deck and lined up in two rows for inspection by the buyers. The hardship of the past weeks had laid most of us so low we looked a truly pitiful sight; clothes dirty and cheeks pale and thin from lack of nourishment. Three or four men, who we later discovered were planters, walked amongst us and ordered some to lift up their arms or open their mouths and in short treating them just like cattle to be bought at market'.

'Soon the salesman for the agent called their attention to him and began to invite bids for

the first unfortunate. He read out the first name saying "stand forth Richard Daniel. Come gentlemen who will start the bidding; he may look weak but not so much as he looks. I'll warrant a good cut or two of the whip will encourage some enthusiasm out of him. Who bids for this man". After a little interest he was sold for the paltry sum of five pounds. The sale lasted a couple of hours with us all being knocked down for amounts that did vary greatly. Next we were marched off to the quayside where an important person in great wig and black coat read out the laws now governing our servitude much of which relied upon punishment by whipping, pillory or stocks. By some good providence we realised that several of us from Colyton were bought by the same master which helped to give us courage and strength for the unknown'.

There are gaps in records but as far as is possible to establish, Peter Bagwell, Peter Ticken, William Greenaway and John Heathfield were sold to Nicholas Maynard, John Whicker and Richard Daniel sold to Charles Thomas & Co, John Moggridge sold to Elizabeth Foster, Robert Sands sold to John Goldingham, John Facey sold to Michael Child and Benjamin Whicker sold to Barnabas Chater. John Truen and George Macey to Capt. Walter Scott. William Marthers died after arrival but before being sold, whilst Bernard Lowman's ending is unknown.

'We were then formed up to march from the port and, after what seemed a considerable distance to our weak bodies, arrived at our new master's estate. Next we were herded towards a kind of village with a double row of huts forming a broad street. They looked more like pigsties for size and shape being built of sticks with plantain leaves both for sides and roofs. No sign of chimney or windows and some had no doors but just an opening; here was realisation that this might prove to be our home for the next ten years. Inside we discovered simple beds made out of pallets and the most basic equipment of plate and basin; most seemed prepared for four occupants in such small space'.

'We'd not been there for long before we were all called outside and once more lined up in front of a man we'd learn to fear. Almost his first words was how he'd get his money's worth from us or would cut us all to pieces and all this time his overseers stood by cracking their whips to cower any brave enough to respond. It wasn't long before we discovered he was drunkard, profligate and blasphemer with no compassion in his body whatsoever'.

BY THE Rt.Hon. THE LIEUT. GOVERNOR OF BARBADOS

Captain James May commander of the ship Betty, John Penne,John Maddison mate, Gabriel Whithorn boatswain and Malcum Fraser doctor of the ship, personally appeared before me and made oath on the Holy Evangelists of Almighty God, that the within servants or convicted rebels by the said May taken in at the port of Weymouth in the county of Dorsett, are the very same convicted rebels that were delivered to, and by the said May brought in the said ship to this island, and that they were all of them here landed and delivered to Mr Charles Thomas and Company Factors to Jerome Nepho or his assignees except eight of them which dyed on board the said ship in the voyage, and buried in the sea, whose names are mentioned in the within Bill of Mortality. Given under my hand the 8ᵗʰ day of January 1686

Edwyn Stede
Lieutenant Governor

(Another copy of the above included: 'except one of the said rebels by name of William Mader (possibly Marthers) that died on shore since the arrival of the said ship'.)

On October 11ᵗʰ 1685 the King had circulated a letter to all island governors with clear orders, that under no circumstances, should any arriving rebel convict be allowed to free themselves in or by any manner. Any trying to do so or any helping in such attempt to suffer the severest punishment. On December 29ᵗʰ the letter was read in the council at Barbados and a committee of four was appointed to draw up a statute conforming to the royal requirements. This act went into the most amazing and comprehensive detail covering the restrictions to be imposed upon the rebels and penalties on them or anyone providing help, assistance or comfort of any kind. It was passed on January 4ᵗʰ 1686 and, when read in full, must be one of the cleverest and most devious legislations ever produced.

We do know what happened to the other Colyton rebels, not in the main group and subject to different arrangements and transactions. John Bagwell, John Marwood and George Robertson were being shipped on the 'Jamaica

Merchant' captained by Charles Gardner bound for Jamaica on behalf of Sir Christopher Musgrave. George Macey was one of Sir William Booth's convicts also shipped out of Weymouth, but bound for Barbados on the 'Happy Return' captained by James Kendall and, on arrival, delivered to John Moore & Co who sold him to plantation owner Capt Walter Scott.

John Skiffes, Argentine Rust and Richard Willmott, tried at Wells and on Sir Phillip Howard's list, were sent to Jamaica on the 'Port Royal'. Francis Bagwell was amongst Sir William Stapleton's batch on the 'Endeavour' from Bristol to Nevis. From other accounts, it seems those sent to Jamaica received better and more sympathetic treatment than the fate of those on Barbados, where the regime was without doubt the hardest.

PLANTATION LIFE FOR A SLAVE

Acting on the King's instructions the Governor of Barbados issued a long and detailed proclamation concerning the captivity and employment of the rebels. It was clearly intended to ensure that they received no help or sympathy from anyone resident on the island or they too would suffer the consequences.

As punishment for 'their late and wicked inhuman and damnable rebellion' they were to serve the full ten years of their sentence, with no possibility of remission whatsoever. They were obliged 'to carry out all such labour and services as they shall be commanded to perform by their masters, owners, mistresses or overseers'. The secretary to the governor was ordered to keep an up-to-date list of all the felons on the island and no one would be allowed to leave Barbados without a ticket or passport, which could only be issued after such list was checked. If any convicted rebel was caught trying to escape secretly from the island 'he would be given thirty nine lashes on his body, set in a pillory, and 'FT' branded upon his forehead with a hot iron for 'fugitive traitor'.

The proclamation also attempted to close down any practical means by which an attempt to escape might be made. It ordered every keeper of a boat or vessel to register it with the local magistrates and lodge a bond of £200. He would forfeit this sum if any 'servant' used his vessel to get away from the island with or without permission or knowledge. Any attempt or thoughts of a shrewd marriage would not help a convict rebel to shorten his punishment. Should he try to obtain remission by marrying a local woman and changing his status from rebel to citizen, his ownership would be shifted to a new master immediately. The woman who had married him would be fined £200 and suffer six months imprisonment for her action. Similarly any person giving consent to any such marriage of their daughter or other relation would suffer in the same manner.

Life for the rebels would have been extremely hard as Peter might relate so let him continue:

'I soon formed the opinion the Negroes may be better off than we white slaves for they had a lifetime of service to provide and therefore treated and viewed as being of more value much as you might cattle. On the other hand he owned we whites for no more than ten years and would therefore push to get the most work and value for his outlay regardless of the cost to each of us as individuals. For food we were allowed an allowance of five pounds of salt beef which was so tough and leathery no end of boiling would make it soft enough for our teeth to tackle. Ground Indian corn was made into a kind of porridge called loblollie, which was the staple of food.'

'Another difficulty to get used to were the cockroaches, great spiders, horrid scorpions, centipedes and lizards. There are ants which swarm everywhere and clouds of flies whilst at night there are moskeetos and merrywings which by their bite are known to drive a newcomer into fever or a kind of madness'.

'If all this were not enough we were woken before daybreak to work in the fields until eleven o'clock when we stopped for a lunch of sorts until staring again at one o'clock until six o'clock of the evening'.

All the rebel prisoners were put to work on the plantations and as they quickly discovered any misbehaviour or failure to satisfy their masters resulted in a beating by whip or cane. Many other similar abuses and unkindnesses were regularly inflected upon them, some meted out on a whim of master or overseer. Anyone now in ownership of a rebel, who was to release or help him in any way, would be fined at least £200 and imprisoned for a year. Such harsh laws were an ingenious and undeniably effective way of ensuring loyalty and obedience by all involved.

King James would have been only too well aware that field labour in the plantations was potential death to most Europeans unused to the climate and conditions. Life was unbearable working without shade during the hot days and led to illness and great suffering; the prevalence of yellow fever threatened many. Conditions were appalling, with men continuing to be bought and sold from one planter to another, some to be attached to work like horses at a grinding wheel whilst others whipped at the post and being forced to sleep like hogs.

The 'plantation colonies', which produced export crops such as sugar and tobacco to meet an increasing demand in Europe, were expanding fast. The early plantation labourers were white men but, by now, the trading nations

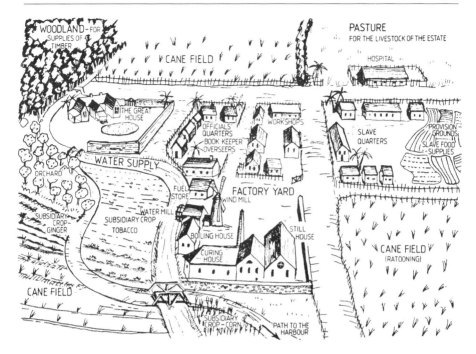

Typical plantation layout

of England, Holland and France had begun to carry slaves from Africa to America and black labourers were in greater number than white. However, it was white men who were increasingly needed for more skilled jobs such as smiths, masons and the like. The arrival of our rebels, who possessed a variety of skills and trades and were able to think for themselves, was most fortunate. Due to this chronic shortage of skilled labour some of the luckier whites managed to escape the work gangs in the cane fields and, instead, became trained as boilers, distillers, refiners and, sometimes eventually as overseers.

It may be surprising to learn that letters, to and from home, did get through to the prisoners as demonstrated by one from a friend of Peter Bagwell. Fellow rebel, Thomas Frankling of Luppitt, wrote from Barbados dated June 1st 1686 bearing witness to this fact:

Dearest and ever loving wife my heartfelt love to
you and to my children, hoping in God…….will find
you and my children all in good health as I am at the
present writing, for which I have great reason to
bless God for it, for out of sixtie of our men
that……come to this island…….I having sent four letters
before this which I make no doubt but that some of
them did come to your hands. Peter Bagwell and John
Whicker have had a letter of ……….to John Whicker
from his father, and Peter from Sarah Tomson which
makes me wonder that you did neglect or that you
cannot find any way to send me a line or two to
satisfy me how it is with you, and to know whether
there are any hopes for my redemption for I did
understand Peter Bagwell's letter that there was
some hope of deliverance if it…..well looked after.

So wife, I would desire that you would guard your
(words or tongue) that I might again enjoy the….. of
my wife and childrens and relations in good old
England as formerly I have…….and if it may be the
will of God to have it, so in short my kind and
heartie love to all my friends and relations. So all
at present but preferring to ……….you and my children,
and all to the protection of the almightie whom I
hope and trust will provide for you both spiritually
and materially.

So I remain your ever tried and faithful husband
until death.

(signed) *Thomas Frankling*

*The original is in the hands of John Whicker's American descendants. The gaps are
due to the age and deterioration of the paper upon which it was written.*

All of the West Indies group of islands had become colonised by a mixture
of Dutch, French and English. The latter possessed a fairly compact group
of islands in the middle of the arc and are known as the Leeward Islands -
the four chief settlements were Antigua, Montserrat, Nevis and part of St.
Kitts (shared with the French). However, Barbados was the largest British

colony of about 166 square miles compared to St.Kitts of 65 and Nevis only 50 (the Isle of Wight is 145).

Sugarcane was planted in holes or trenches made by the hoe and grew for fourteen to eighteen months or until it was as high as a man. It was cut down with billhooks and knives and carried into the mill. This might be worked by wind, water or cattle. The mill ground the juice out of the cane until it flowed along a pipe to the boiling house. There it was boiled and skimmed until it was ready to 'strike' or crystallize. Then it was ladled into a cooler from which it was transferred into pots with holes in the bottom. There it stood whilst the coarse brown crystals of the Muscovado sugar separated from the viscous part which would not crystallize; this was the molasses; it dripped out of the pots and was collected to be consumed or exported or boiled up again into second rate sugar or, most often, distilled into rum. The Muscovado sugar stood thus for some time in the curing house and was then barreled up into hogsheads, or smaller barrels, carted down to the port and loaded aboard ship bound for England and the rich merchants.

ESCAPE FROM SLAVERY

Gradually men made friendships and inevitably talk of escape became uppermost in some minds and here we meet Henry Pitman from Yeovil. He was a Doctor of Medicine, who had the greatest of misfortune to have got caught up in the rebellion only due to 'coming upon the aftermath of battle and feeling obliged to tend men's wounds at Sedgemoor'. He, together with his brother William, had arrived with the Colyton men on 'The Betty' but, due to the ill treatment everyone was subjected to, his brother had died.

Early in 1687, he became determined to hatch a plan for a daring escape and sought out a few men who he felt could be trusted and who were prepared to risk their lives in search of freedom (yet again!). First he approached a debtor (not a rebel) John Nuthall, who needed money to secure his own release. After discussion, Pitman gave him £7 to pay off his debt and £12 to buy a boat. Nuthall, whilst grateful, was also most nervous and reported that magistrates had become inquisitive about his owning a vessel. Fearing discovery Pitman instructed him to sink the boat to avoid further question and investigation.

Other crew would be needed so Pitman sought out other volunteers and, swearing them to secrecy, outlined his plans to Peter Bagwell and John Whicker. Both chose to join him without hesitation and before long five others were enlisted as crew. By the end of April plans well advanced and a hidden store of supplies building up. By their departure these included a hundredweight of bread, cheese, cask of water, bottles of Canary★ and Madeira wine and beer. A compass, a quadrant, chart, half hour glass, half-minute glass, log and line, tarpaulin, hatchet, hammer and nails, spare boards, lantern and candles.

It was known that on the 9th May 1687 the Governor of Barbados would be entertaining the Governor of Nevis. It would almost certainly mean celebrations taking place amongst the soldiers resulting in a slackening of

★   a light sweet wine from the Canary Islands

security, due to feasting, revelling and drinking to excess. It seemed the perfect night to choose to make their escape. At around 11pm. they silently pushed their small craft from land and paddled away. The intention was to head for the Dutch-held island of Curacao about 200 leagues (600 miles) away where they felt they would be received with some sympathy. Once out in the open seas it wasn't long before they realized the poor circumstances of their position. The boat leaked freely requiring them to make immediate attempts at plugging the holes with rags and candle grease. There was a need to constantly bail out which only served to increase the danger of increasing weakness from poor diet and exhaustion fast set in.

Come the morning of the 10th they were almost out of sight of Barbados so they hoisted the sail and a course was set southwest towards Great Granada. Soon sea sickness added to their discomfort and their limited supply of fresh water was being used up more quickly than expected. At one time they lost overboard a wooden bowl, their only baling implement, and were unable to retrieve it, which served to increase their jeopardy still more. Their candles and matches were damp so that night they lived in the hope

of being safely guided by the stars. Worse was to come as that night the rudder split and they were forced to steer with an oar.

During the night of 12/13th May they passed Great Grenada which served as a considerable encouragement and lifted their spirits. It seems none aboard were able to use the navigation equipment so they hopped from island to island as best their chart could tell them, now setting course for the Testigos.

By noon on the 14th the Testigos was spotted and by nightfall the tip of Margarita was in their sight. The temptation to put in for rest and shelter persuaded them to head inwards but on getting closer they spotted what they feared to be Indian cannibals on the shoreline and immediately rowed away. Tiredness, fear and uncertainty were once again their unseen but constantly present companions.

During the day of the 15th it was decided that the north side of the island appeared uninhabited so were persuaded to once more try putting ashore.

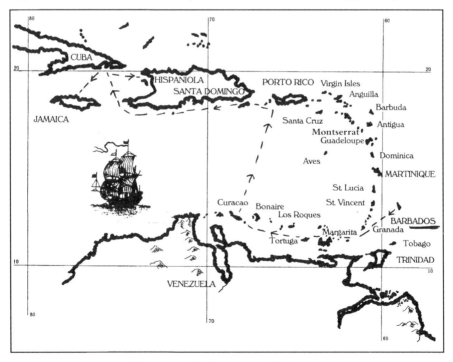

The route of their escape and adventure

The tide ran onto the rocks so fast they were threatened with being crushed to matchsticks and it was only by luck they fended themselves off and once more found reserves of strength to row themselves away and out of immediate danger.

Now a course for Saltatudos* was set but once more the sea displayed its anger and they found themselves caught up in a great storm which threatened to capsize and wreck the vessel. Constantly lashed by wind and rain and fears of never seeing the next morning's sun, they prayed to God that he should command the violence of the winds to cease and allay the fury of the waves. By daybreak on the 16th they had the island of Saltatudos in their sights and as they neared the shore to their surprise a canoe was spotted paddling out to meet them. Alarmed by this John and Peter, who had managed to bring muskets but in their hurry had left a bag of bullets on the Barbados wharf, charged their guns with glass. Before needing to discharge their load it became apparent that those approaching were white men and were now close enough to enquire of them who they were. 'Englishmen in distress and waiting for a chance to get off the island', they replied led the rebels into shore.

Imagine their surprise to discover they had come upon a band of English Privateers (more like buccaneers) whose occupation was to sail round the islands seeking ships to plunder. They refreshed themselves with most welcome water from a well and after being given food took themselves to rest, sleep and recover from their hard voyage.

The captain and crew treated them well and, as you would expect, each side exchanged stories of their experiences. The next day Henry, John and Peter inspected their boat with a view to sealing the leaks and erecting a better cover for shelter from the wind and sea spray in order to continue their journey. Observing this activity their new-found companions tried to persuade our rebels to join them in their piracy but Henry, on behalf of the others, steadfastly refused. Believing it might persuade them to change their minds, the privateers burned their boat and sails. However, Henry remained determined not to join them but realizing the difficulty of their position offered 30 Pieces of Eight for an Indian who had been captured by the

---

* The English named it because of the plentiful supply of salt to be found on the island whilst the Spaniards called it Tortuga from the turtles inhabiting it.

privateers. His ability to catch fish and find food sources might prove invaluable to their survival as time went on. Finally, on the 25th May, just sixteen days after their escape from Barbados, our rebels watched them depart from the island.

This left them deserted, shipwrecked and stranded on the island which they now knew the Spaniards claimed and had named it Tortuga, with no means to leave unless another ship should come along. It must have seemed they had exchanged one captivity for another and feared for their survival. The island was uninhabited so, together with their Indian, they had to search out and discover foods and water supplies to sustain them so that their bodies hardened to the sun and their feet toughened by clambering over rocks.

'Turning turtle'

In resourceful fashion they made themselves huts of grass and for the next three months lived mainly on turtle meat, turtle eggs, fish, young birds and wild vegetables. In the morning they would go down to the shoreline and turn the turtles onto their backs to immobilize them for collection later. Not surprisingly this diet caused great looseness of the bowels requiring treatment by opium pills from the doctor's medical supplies.

By extracting fibres from some plant leaves it was possible produce a thread of sorts which, when used with needles of bone, allowed the mending of clothes. The fruit of prickly pear made a spirituous liquor to drink and they smoked wild sage, in place of tobacco, in pipes made of crab claws. Henry Pitman's own written account provides great detail of quite amazing resourcefulness employed by them all.

In August, after being marooned for some three months on Saltatudos, a ship together with a small sloop put in towards their island. With mixed hope it would be an English vessel and fear in case it were Spaniards bound to make them prisoners they watched it come into anchor. It turned out be another English privateer, which encouraged thoughts of rescue. On learning one of the castaways was a doctor they invited Henry aboard and during the visit he learned the sloop with them was a captured 'prize', which they were taking into port. Henry asked passage for both he and his companions to the port or transfer to another friendly vessel should they come upon one. Unfortunately the captain and crew had a shared financial interest and were only prepared to take the doctor, presumably viewing his profession as of some use to them.

Imagine the feelings John, Peter and others would have had in learning they were not to be included in the rescue. Their plight was slightly eased by supplies of wine, bread, cheese, bacon and other useful bits being given them. Thus our rebels were left behind with an uncertain future hoping a friendly ship would come by before too long and provide them with the means for them also to finally reach safety.

The story continues to be really quite extraordinary and undoubtedly the best person to tell the story is John Whicker who had assumed leadership of the group. On his eventual safe return to England he wrote a letter to Henry Pitman, at his request, giving an account of the experiences after they had parted company:

Dear Doctor,
In answer to your request, I have given you the following account.
About a fortnight after you left us on Saltatudos [*in August,1687*], two of our companions, JOHN NUTHALL and THOMAS WAKER [*the two that had not been out with MONMOUTH*], having made sails of the cloth the privateers left us, and fitted the Spanish boat for the sea, went from us, designing for Curacoa. But the boat was so large and unruly, and they, so unskilful in navigation; that I fear they either perished in the sea, or were driven ashore on the Main among the cruel Spaniards: for we never heard of them since.

From the pages of this letter, which follows, we learn there was a falling out amongst the crew of the ship with which Henry had sailed resulting in nine of them being put ashore on an island to fend for themselves. Somehow they were able to make their way by boat towards Tobago but unintentionally ended up on the far side of Saltatudos where John and the others were marooned. Between them more argument took place resulting in three making prisoners of the others and keeping them short of food. One of them managed to escape his bonds and fled the camp in search of food and water, which is when he stumbled into the rebel's camp and sought their help.

What followed for the next six months was to include capture by Spanish pirates, made prisoners and forced to work as slaves. John continues his story:

Being thus exiled from his companions, he bethought himself of ranging the island to look for men: for the turtle which they had found came afresh in his memory. All this time he had no victuals, nor a drop of water, being excessively hot.

At length, having travelled about the island till almost ready to faint; he came near our huts; and seeing us dressing of turtle with nothing on but a pair of drawers, the man made a stand, thinking we had been Indians, for we were tanned with the sun almost as yellow as them.

At length, he advanced, and enquired if we were Englishmen?

We told him, "We were." Then he begged for a little water, which we gave him, and some of our turtle.

And after some conference, he told us of his condition, and desired us to help him to regain what was so ungratefully taken from him and his fellow sufferers, by their own countrymen and boats crew. Which we readily agreed to.

And when we had fixed our arms, we travelled all night till we came where the boat lay, which was about six or seven miles from that place.

When we came near the place, we hid ourselves in the bushes by the seaside, waiting their coming ashore next morning, which they usually did, as we were informed.

Morning being come; two of them came ashore, and the Negro slave bearing a vessel to fetch water: they with their arms, and leaving one aboard, with twelve pieces by him ready loaded.

When they were come ashore, we appeared, with our arms ready cocked, enclosed them and took them prisoners.

Then we brought them to the water-side, and shewed the other aboard what we had done, commanding him not to fire, but to jump overboard, and swim ashore to us: which he immediately did.

So taking them all three prisoners we put them ashore, leaving them some of our provisions.

The rest we put aboard, in order to prosecute our voyage for New England. So victualling and watering our small frigate in the best manner we could, we left them upon the island, and the 24th of August [1687] we took our departure from Saltatudos.

In about six days time we made the island of Porto Rico, But our pilot not being very well acquainted with that country, supposed it to be the high land of Santo Domingo upon Hispaniola; and therefore ordered to bear up the helm and stand away to the westward before the wind.

The next day, we could see no land, which caused no small trouble amongst us, being dubious where we were.

Towards the evening we made the east end of Hispaniola. Then our pilot saw his error, and that we had lost our passage between the islands Hispaniola and Porto Rico.

......We were sailing down the south side of Hispaniola about nine days, having some times very little wind, and at other times tornadoes that we could carry no sail. Our water was all spent.

Running along close aboard the shore, we espied three men running with all the haste that possibly they could, till they came to a canoe which lay at the mouth of a creek, which immediately they rowed up into the country among the woods. We imagined they were afraid of us, supposing us to be Spaniards.

Then we came to an anchor and I myself with one more, a carpenter, swam ashore: but with a great deal of difficulty, for the rocks lying so far off the shore, had like to have dashed out our brains.

Coming ashore, we swam up the creek; but the tide being so strong against us, we were forced to return back again, neither finding the men nor hope of getting fresh water. Therefore we swam aboard again.

Weighing our anchor, we steered within the isle of Ash, which lies almost to the west end of Hispaniola. Our pilot looking over his Waggoner, found that within this island was a fresh-water creek, into which we designed to run; but through mistake ran about two leagues up into a wrong creek where we could find no fresh water: so that with drinking salt water, our mouths were almost grown together and hardly able to speak.

But GOD Almighty was pleased to send us a very great shower of rain, which lasted so long that, by means of a sheet held up by the four corners with a weight in it, we caught about two gallons of water.

So lowering our sails we hauled up the creek into the woods, and went ashore, and concluded to dig a well. When we had digged about four or six feet deep, we found fresh water to our great comfort and satisfaction.

Lying ashore all night to take up the water as it sprang, we were almost stung to death with a sort of flies, called *Musquitoes and Merrywings,* which drew blisters and bladders in our skin, that we looked as if we had the smallpox; which were very tedious for our bodies too.

By next morning, we had got about forty gallons of water aboard, with which we put to sea again.

But we had not been at sea above three hours, before we saw a sail within the west end of the isle of Ash before mentioned. We bore up our helm and stood away for her. In a short, time we saw her come to an anchor.

Supposing to be a Jamaica sloop, for she had our king's Jack *[arms}* and ancient *[colours};* we hailed them.

Whose answer was "From Jamaica"

So coming to anchor by their side, they lain us aboard with two canoes, full of Spaniards, all armed as pirates, and carried us aboard their sloop, stripped us naked, and put us down in their hold: having nothing to lay our naked bodies upon but their ballast stones, or atop of their water cask.

The provisions they allowed us were course and short: about half a pint of Indian corn a day for a man, for nine days together.

The place where they carried us is called St. Jago, a Spanish town upon Cuba.

We remained in this condition above six months. When they went to sea, we were carried as their slaves, to pump ship, wash their clothes, and beat corn in great wooden mortars; with Negroes, with naked swords, always standing by us as overseers: so that our hands had been bladdered, and so sore that we could hardly hold anything. When at home, our business was to row the canoe up two leagues into the country, full of jars, to fetch water, which we were forced to carry upon our naked backs a great way, to fill them, sometimes, into the woods to cut wood, bare footed and bare legged, with neither a shirt to our hack, nor a hat to our head, but only a rag sufficient to cover our nakedness. Our provisions, as I told you before, were Indian corn boiled in water; but a larger share than the first.

About the latter end of October [1687], we were divided: myself with three more were put on board a small bark, the rest of my companions remained aboard the sloop; both vessels being bound down to leeward off Cape [de] Cruz; having information of a Dutch trader that lay there, before a small town, called Byan.

In which voyage, we were taken very sick in the ague, as well Spaniards as English; which reduced us to a deplorable condition, having nothing to yield us any comfort.

In this distemper, died one of our companions, JEREMIAH ATK1NS, of Taunton. During his sickness, they were very cruel to him; not suffering us to carry him down into the hold, but made him lie day and night upon the deck. All we could do for him, was to cover him with the bark of a cabbage tree, to keep the sun from him by day, and the dew by night. In this languishing condition, he lay about a week; and then died. When dead, they threw him overboard, letting him float astern; without using any means to sink him, as is usual.

Returning back again for St. Jago without their expected prize; myself and one more of our companions were taken again from on board the bark, and put aboard the sloop, and two others of our English were put aboard the bark, which took its departure from us at Cape [de] Cruz aforesaid, bound for Cartagena, a Spanish town upon the main continent.

In five days, we arrived at our port of St. Jago, where we lay about a month.

Having careened our sloop, we put to sea again, bound for the north side of Hispaniola, to take Frenchmen.

Turning up to windward of Cuba, we met with a Jamaica sloop bound for the Wrack. The Spaniard commanded him to hoist out his canoe and come aboard: which he refusing went his way.

Having weathered Cape Myceze [*Maysi*], which is the eastward point of Cuba, we stood along shore, bound for a small town, called Barracco [*Baracoa*], where in two days we arrived.

We lay there till the latter end of October, [1687], at which place our sloop drave ashore, and struck off about fourteen feet of the false keel: but after a great of trouble, we got her off again. At this place, they got two hogs; and a quantity of plantains, a sort of food that grow upon trees, and are made use of instead of bread, among the inhabitants in the West Indies.

We then proceeded in our voyage for Hispaniola, and fell in with a place called the Mould. Off which place, we saw two sail: an English vessel that came from Jamaica, bound for New York, and a French sloop bound for Petty Guavas, a French town to leeward, on the north side of the said Hispaniola.

Having a fresh gale, we came up with the Englishman, brought him by the lee, commanded the Captain with four of his men aboard, and put twelve Spaniards aboard his ship.

Then chasing the Frenchman we came up with him, about an hour after night. The Frenchman stood it out and fought us, making a stout resistance, although they had not above seven or eight men, and of the Spaniards, their were thirty-five men, eight guns, six patteroes, and every man his small arms. The French making such a bold resistance kept them off till such time as they had an opportunity to run their sloop aground in the Mould in the dark, by which means they saved their lives: otherwise they had been all dead men, as the Spaniards swore if they took them.

In the next morning, we ran into the Mould, and brought out their sloop, and put about ten men aboard: bringing both prizes away for St. Jago.

From the English Captain they took £900 in money, and plundered him of all he had, save a suit of clothes that he wore: and but waited the governor's [of St. Jago} motion to make a prize of the ship. Which would have been done had not the Spanish Governor received advice of the Duke of ALBEMARLE's arrival at Jamaica.

Upon which news, the Governor paid the English Captain £600 of his money back again, and sent him away to Jamaica, and all the English prisoners, that would go with him were freed by his consent.

By this time, arrived the bark in which were the other three of our companions; who were very glad to hear of our and their redemption.

We embarked once again free men together, by god's grace, bound for Jamaica: where we safely arrived about the latter end of March [1688].

So separating ourselves, we endeavoured in the best manner we could to get passage for England, our native country, desiring GOD Almighty to deliver us, and all our dear countrymen Protestants, from the barbarous cruelty of the Spaniards and Papists.

John Whicker 1688

After a trip via Puerto Rico and Hispaniola Henry Pitman was landed in Carolina on the American mainland. Finding no vessel bound directly for England he gained a passage to New York and eventually one whose destination was Amsterdam. About five weeks later it arrived at Cowes on the Isle of Wight from where he crossed to Southampton at the end of an amazing journey.

From his lodgings at the sign of the Ship in Paul's Churchyard, London Dr Henry Pitman wrote and published a narrative of his experiences entitled 'A Relation of the Great Sufferings and Strange Adventures of Henry Pitman' dated June 10th 1689.

What interesting comparisons can be made with the story of Robinson Crusoe by Daniel Defoe published some years later in 1719. Defoe was a dissenter, something of a rebel and is believed to have taken up with Monmouth's campaign.

Meanwhile back on Barbados and Jamaica those rebels still surviving became settled into and accepting of their new life in the colonies but in England James II was making himself seriously unpopular. Disregarding popular opinion he actively encouraged the appointment of Catholics into the most senior positions of authority in all areas of English life. This was clearly unacceptable and led to those of influence, and combined in their opposition, to invite the King's Protestant son in law, William of Orange, to land and claim the throne of England in 1688. William landed in Torbay and marched on London encountering no opposition with the army and navy deserting to him and finding the Duke of Marlborough on his side. James fled to France and Judge Jeffreys made a quick departure from London to seek a ship to the Continent but was recognized, arrested and later executed

King William may well have been prepared to recognize he had no moral right to keep the rebels in servitude. In many ways they had been his vanguard paving the way for his opportunity now taken. On July 3rd 1689 the Lords of Trade sought instructions to clarify the position of those prisoners in the West Indies. Unhappy at the prospect of losing skilled white labour there was a howl of protest from plantation owners when they heard a pardon was rumoured. Much lobbying took place which resulted, on 20th November 1690, in new instructions being sent to the colonies providing that 'acts should be passed repealing the prisoners servitude for ten years but reimposing such conditions as might be necessary to keep them in the islands until the King should permit them to leave'.

The Council of Barbados duly passed an act on March 17th stating that all the prisoners should be liable for military service until released from such obligation by the King. This would appear to have been a clever device influenced by the plantation owners to avoid releasing them and the same laws for escape remained in force. It is not hard to imagine how the plantation owners felt cheated having, from their point of view, paid good money to obtain ten years service from each man. The rebels had become well trained, proficient at their work and a welcome addition to the workforce so the prospect of releasing any of them was not welcomed. As reported by the Governor of Barbados, many deaths had occurred amongst these white servants so many less were remaining alive to benefit from the political change and pardon.

Meanwhile back in England court records show that in May 1689 a petition was submitted by John Clapp (who you'll remember had got back safely to Colyton and hid in the roof), Joseph Pitts, John Gould of Colyton and Nathaniel Smith of Honiton that:

> the following persons, men of industrious and sober lines, who were sentenced to be sold as slaves to America, be allowed to return home to their families. All were taken into custody after the defeat of The Duke of Monmouth, some having taken up arms against the king, others having supplied provisions to the rebels, but many not having associated at all. Judge Jeffreys required all of them to plead guilty or face immediate execution and they were therefore terrified into making false confessions and accepting banishment for ten years, - viz, Benjamin Whicker, Gideon Dare, John Bagwell, George Macey, Richard Parker and Nicholas Salter.

Another report of this petition includes the additional names of Argentine Rust and John Heathfield.

However, little happened so they enlisted the help of Sir Walter Yonge who, during 1690, helped to persuade King William to announce a proper pardon and recall the men transported abroad back to their homes in England. His intervention and willingness to help must be viewed as interesting and goes some way to reassure us that his support for 'the cause', and those who supported it, remained strong.

Realism makes us recognize that many of those who toiled under the hot sun failed to make it home. The numbers who did is uncertain as, by this time, many had perished, some of whom succumbed to the peril of yellow fever or maybe were clever enough to escape. Certainly once they became free the rebels in Barbados found the authorities had no intention of providing help for them to return home. If they could not pay for a passage then their only other hope was to find a place as a crew member and work their way back to England. Perhaps some, like others, had money sent from relatives in Colyton. Some did choose to start a new life and remain on Barbados or one of the other islands, preferring the warm climate they had managed to get used to rather than the prospect of cold wet winters and drudgery of ploughing or wool combing in the Coly Valley.

In all probability less than a quarter of all the rebel prisoners returned to England. Those remaining constructed cabins and homes of dry stone not unlike those found in the West Country. Locally these inhabitants became known as Redlegs or Redshanks, which was in reference to their sunburned legs. Females from English Poor Houses were later shipped to the island and this eventually was to enable them to keep their community white.

IN CONCLUSION

For 105 men to leave their homes, farms and workplaces within a few days and rise up for Monmouth surely needed a decision to have been in place for some while. They must have had great confidence that their 'Protestant Duke' would come and raise his banner to champion their Protestant religion and freedom.

For weeks or maybe months Roger Satchell, and the others in the forefront of planning, must have been gathering together their arms and supplies in readiness to react quickly when the call came. Messages, relating to the preparations taking place in Holland and the imminent invasion, filtered in through the port of Lyme to be delivered to the trusted few. They in turn would secretly pass the word to those they could trust. Many men and families from the communities of Lyme and Colyton had daily or weekly contact, trading and talking together, keeping each other up to date with local news and national developments. There can be little doubt, without such planning, it is unlikely such large numbers of men would have been in a position to have taken their leave of homes and families within a couple of days. Understandings and arrangements had to have been in place between husband and wives, brothers and cousins for life and work to be carried on.

Monmouth's was a voluntary army with no pressure applied to anyone to join. It is unlikely they were drawn into rebellion by economic grievances, for the valley had a modest prosperity. Whilst not well off, they hadn't the need to fight for a higher standard of living, just their religious and traditional liberties. Admittedly five or more years before there had been unemployment in the wool trade with changing markets but by this time it, and agriculture, were doing quite well again

History records it as the Monmouth Rebellion but in truth it was the People's Rebellion and only a long time coming because a leader was needed through whom their anger, fears and resentments could be harnessed and expressed.

Quite ordinary men went off to fight for their beliefs and, in most cases probably thought sheer force of their numbers was going to ensure their success. The use of force and arms was probably not believed as necessary to many a man who would normally have spent his time in the field or working his craft and certainly with no experience of fighting. It really was a pitchfork rebellion not because it was made up of peasants but because of the very real lack of and make-do manner of weapons amongst many of the rebel force.

Most of the rank and file to form the rebel army possessed no great political thoughts save wanting to be ruled by parliament not an absolute king. They recognized the need for a social hierarchy and could accept an elected seat of power occupied by merchants, gentlemen and lawyers as parliament was meant to be. A strong independence of view had developed which easily converted to out and out opposition once pushed too far. Many were referred to as true democrats, they believed that there was no man born marked of God above another; 'for none comes into the world with a saddle on his back, neither booted and spurred to ride him'. Men who believed that shopkeepers, artisan and farmers like themselves had as good a right to rule the land as the greatest lord in the kingdom.

Undoubtedly Colyton was devastated by the events in the aftermath of Monmouth's landing at Lyme Regis. The effect on most southwest communities must have been indescribable causing them to feel threatened by any attempt to write or record the happenings outside of the official line and propaganda at the time. What they could never forget was the suffering and terror inflicted upon them in defeat. Legends and stories built up and inevitably some facts may become confused in their telling and retelling. Some virtually innocent men were accused, found guilty and sentenced. Even people without any sympathy for the rebellion were horrified at the barbarity of reprisal meted out at the "Bloody Assizes".

By law 'a subject attainted of treason shall forfeit all his substance' and this was enforced after the trials with a cruel rigour. Broken hearted widows and destitute orphans of the men whose corpses hung at cross roads were forced to give up property and possessions by treasury officials in a manner most felt amounted to little more than 'legal pillage'. Without doubt some were often forced to resort to begging as is recorded by the plight of Phillip Cox's wife. Despite everything she felt he had nobly given his life in God's cause and, like others, in the bible she sought solace. It was written that, in her moments of mourning, the words in Ecclesiastes might come to mind:

'to everything a season, and a time and purpose under heaven'.

The general Pardon of March 1686 allowed men on the run or in hiding to return to their homes. Not only had individual families suffered great loss but local economies were damaged. The massacre, hangings and transportation were a disaster for the whole town as they destroyed a large number of useful craftsmen and skilled labourers. Some rebels who had escaped to the Continent, and using their skills, now began to set up in the cloth trade in competition to that in England. King James, unable to ignore the still remaining importance to the export trade, realised action was needed to reduce this economic threat. This encouraged him to offer pardons and by June 1686 most had accepted and closed their looms down and slowly returned home.

THOSE REBELS WHO MADE IT HOME TO COLYTON

A search of Colyton Parish records provides a lot of information when trying to identify who made it home to the town. Of the twenty-three Colyton rebels transported only the following seven have been identified as safely returned: John Skiffes was back from Jamaica by 1693 and had a child baptised in Colyton the following summer and another in 1697. Peter Bagwell died in Colyton in 1693, Robert Sandy married Anne Crow in Sept 1699 and Roger French was buried in Colyton in 1698. As a result of the petition already described it seems only Benjamin Whicker arrived home in Colyton before summer of 1688, got married in 1691 and had 5 children between then and 1710. His escapee brother John got back in the summer of that year and married in 1691 having 7 children between then and 1705.

Others not transported but returned were Bartholomew Butter who died in Colyton 1687; Walter Bagwell, had a son christened in 1688, and died 1695; Edward Barber, had a son baptised 1688, died same year; William Blackmore had a child baptised 1688; Miles Davey jnr had daughters christened in 1694 and 1696; Isaac Drover buried here 1712; Zachary Drover married in Seaton 1691; young John Abrahams had a son baptised 1696; George Farrant, had a son christened 1672, and buried here 1699; John Marwood died 1710; Thomas Teape died 1721; Peter Seller died 1686; John Turner died 1699; Samuel Whicker, had a daughter christened 1691, died 1714.

Rebels granted pardons and assumed would have returned home included Robert Basleigh, John Butcher, Robert Dyer, George Farrant, Thomas Greenaway, Robert Hayman, Nicholas Thompson, George Turner (died 1701) and John Woolmington.

Rebels remaining at large and fate unknown include Amos Bagwell, William Bagwell, William Barnard, James Battins, John Butter, Joshua Cooke, Robert Cooke, Thomas Cox, Ambrose Daniel, John Dare, John Duce, Daniel French, Benedict Hale, Robert and John Halsan, John Hawler, John Hewes, Thomas Leyton, James Lodge, Robert Lucas, Thomas Maxey, William

Mayder, William Mullins, John and Phillip Newton, Jonathan Payne, James Pease, Joseph Pitt, Francis Purchas, John Rowsell, Francis Roberts, William Seaward, 'Soundy', George Spiller, John Stadith, John jnr and snr Toogood, Daniel Toope, William Willsman.

From an original list of 105 rebels only 67 are accounted for leaving us to presume death on the field of battle or that they may have made a successful escape. It is quite certain some took another identity elsewhere in the country or even found a ship bound for somewhere like Virginia where it was known there were Devon folks amongst the English settlements.

There must be families living today who can trace their ancestry back to a rebel and remain to be discovered. One local example is Anne Chapple of Colyford who is able to trace her ancestors through the Restoricks of whom there were three rebels – Joseph, John (1) and John (2). Buildings known as Restorick Row still exists here in Colyton emphasising the connection.

Finally

So there we have it as best I can tell. A story such as this can go on for ever, as indeed does all history, but at some point a line has to be drawn. Doubtless some will find reason to correct me and others to question that which may be missing or not told perfectly. However, I do hope this book may inspire others to delve deeper into their family histories where they suspect a connection may exist with the events featured. In doing so I hope more information may reach me to fill in gaps, expand upon some details or put the record straight. Of particular interest will be the experience and endings of our rebel slaves in the colonies.

Perhaps no revolutionary struggle is totally in vain and the fine and honest citizens of Colyton, who were prepared to stand up and be counted, prepared the way for the peaceful and bloodless arrival of William of Orange and his wife Mary to take the English throne just three years later in 1688.

It seems most appropriate to offer this book as a tribute to the memory of those men.

THE 105 COLYTON MEN LISTED AND ACCUSED OF REBELLION★

Isaac Abrahams
John Abrahams
Amos Bagwell
Francis Bagwell
John Bagwell
Peter Bagwell
Walter Bagwell
William Bagwell
Edward Barber
Wiliam Barnard
Osmond Barrett
Robert Basleigh
James Battins
William Blackmore
William Blackmore
John Butcher
Bartholomew Butter
John Butter
John Clapp
William Clegg,
Joshua Cooke
Robert Cooke
Phillip Cox
Thomas Cox
Ambrose Daniel
Richard Daniel
John Dare
Isaac Drover (Drower)
Zachary Drover (Drower)
John Duce
Robert Dyer
Daniel French
John French
Roger French
John Facey
George Farrant

Thomas Greenaway
William Greenaway
Richard Hall
Robert Hayman
Benedict Hale
Robert Halsan
John Hawler (Hawkier)
John Hewes
John Heathfield
Nicholas Hoare
John Knowles
Percival Knowles
Thomas Layton snr.
James Lodge
Bernard Lowman
Robert Lucas
George Macey
William Marthers
John Marwood
Thomas Maxey
William Mayder
Humphrey Mitchell
John Moggridge
William Mullins
John Newton
Phillip Newton
Jonathan Payne
James Pease
Jospeh Pitt
Francis Purchas
James Pyes
Joseph Restorick
John Rowsell
Francis Roberts
George Robertson
(Robinson)

Argentine Rust
Robert Sands (Sandy,
Sandaway)
Roger Satchell
John Savage
George Seaward (Seward/
Selwood)
William Seaward
Peter Seller (William)
John Skiffes
.........? 'Soundy'
Joseph Speed
George Spiller
John Sprake (Sprague)
John Stadith
John Starr (Starcke)
Robert Teape
Thomas Teape
Nicholas Thompson
Robert Thorne
Peter Ticken (Titchen, Tricker)
John Toogod snr
John Toogod jnr
Daniel Toope
John Truren (Trewron/Truen).
George Turner
John Turner
Edward Venn
Nicholas Warren
Benjamin Whicker
John Whicker (Father)
Samual Whicker senior
Richard Wilmott (Wilmouth)
William Willsman
John Woolmington

★   Taken from Volume 79 Somerset Record Office: The Monmouth Rebels 1685 compiled by
W.Macdonald Wigfield, MA

REBELS FROM VILLAGES NEIGHBOURING COLYTON

It may be of further interest to record this information as, after all, close connections existed between them by way of friendship, trade, labour and family relationships.

Axmouth totalled thirty nine: Bartholomew Baker, Josiah Bartlett (P), Nathaniel Bowditch, Caleb Bragg, William Browne (T), William Brown snr, John Clarke snr, John Clarke jnr (T), George Coade, John Coleman, Joseph Coleman, James Cox, John Cox, Robert Cox, John Deeme, John Forde, Benjamin Gaitch, Joseph Gaitch (T), Walter Gape, Abel Grove, Joseph Hacker, Solomon Hacker, Edward Howard, Abrham Hunt (T), John Lidden, John Limberry, Joseph Limberry, William Limberry, John Lyddon, John Oliver (H), John Quick (T), Robert Quick snr, Robert Quick jnr, William Quick, John Tanner, William Tanner, Walter Teape (T), John White (T), John Wood.

Beer: Edward Parsons, Edward Parsons jnr and John Parsons.

Colyford: John Grace (T) and William Mader.

Kilmington: Thomas Cooke (H) and John White.

Northleigh: Richard Greene.

Musbury totalled twenty five: Ambrose Ashford (T), John Baker, John Bird, Richard Browne, Richard Butcher, Richard Cox, Thomas Cox, William Cox snr (H), William Cox jnr, Richard French, William French, Daniel Hoare, Oliver Hobbes (T), Humphrey Hutchins, Bernard Loveridge, Samual Loveridge, Thomas Loveridge, William Loveridge (T), Robert Rocket, James Salter (T), Aaron Smith, Joseph Standerwick, Edward Trevitt, Peter Willcox.

Seaton: Roger French and Robert Lucas (H).

Whitford: John Bushells, Edward Hooper (shuttlemaker), William Hooper, (T) and William Searle.(T)

Key: T – transported. H – hanged. P – pardoned